J. Wesley Van Dervoort

The Voyage of Life

A journey from the cradle to the grave

J. Wesley Van Dervoort

The Voyage of Life
A journey from the cradle to the grave

ISBN/EAN: 9783744799928

Printed in Europe, USA, Canada, Australia, Japan

Cover: Foto ©Andreas Hilbeck / pixelio.de

More available books at **www.hansebooks.com**

THE

A JOURNEY

From the Cradle to the Grave.

REVISED BY
PROF. J. W. VAN DERVOORT.

ILLUSTRATED.

UNION PUBLISHING HOUSE,
NEW YORK, BOSTON, CINCINNATI, AND ATLANTA, GA.
ACME PUBLISHING HOUSE, CHICAGO.
1883.

Entered according to Act of Congress, in the year 1879, by
J. A. RUTH & CO.,
in the Office of the Librarian of Congress at Washington.

COPYRIGHT, 1882,
By UNION PUBLISHING HOUSE.

INTRODUCTION.

"Your defects to know
Make use of every friend and every foe."

THE title of this book will suggest something of its scope and aim. Life is a fact, and not a glittering generality. The period bounded by its horizons is bristling with great possibilities. The alchemy of success consists in knowing an opportunity when it is met, and what use to make of it. In some sense that lesson will be taught in the following pages. Tender infancy, frolicking childhood, and stern manhood, each with the surroundings incidental to its period, will receive careful consideration. The parents or guardians of youth are exhorted to instill right principles in the minds of their children—to train them to become good citizens. Young men and women are told how to carry out these wise maxims.

Another aim of this book has been to supplant, in some measure, the trashy and pernicious literature of the day, by supplying instead, healthful and inviting food for the mind. It is a compendium of life experience garnered in brief space.

Old age is not always experience. The youth of our land aspire to be greater—all need to be better. We lend a helping hand.

In the preparation of this work, the best thinkers and writers—all available sources of which would add to its merit. and acceptation —have been consulted.

It has been most carefully revised, and nearly one hundred pages of original matter and several new engravings have been added.

The cordial welcome with which the preceding edition has been received, its widespread popularity, induces us to hope that the book in its new and attractive dress will meet with a reception no less flattering.

In the sincere aim to present a volume of solid, instructive and interesting reading matter, especially adapted to the requirements of the home circle, we send "THE VOYAGE OF LIFE" on its mission.

CONTENTS.

		PAGE
I.	THE Voyage of Life	7
II.	Infancy	18
III.	Childhood	26
IV.	The Rights of Children	39
V.	Boys	48
VI.	Girls	60
VII.	Young Men	64
VIII.	Young Women	79
IX.	Brothers and Sisters	94
X.	Man	103
XI.	Woman	110
XII.	Home	121
XIII.	Fathers	136
XIV.	Mothers	149
XV.	Tired Mothers	161
XVI.	Responsibility of Parents	163
XVII.	Amusements	175
XVIII.	Associations	180
XIX.	Friendship	191
XX.	Influence	200
XXI.	Intemperance	209
XXII.	Indolence	220
XXIII.	Integrity	225
XXIV.	Genius	229

		PAGE
XXV.	Ambition vs. Vanity	235
XXVI.	Tact	242
XXVII.	Courage	246
XXVIII.	Economy	252
XXIX.	Industry	260
XXX.	Self-Culture	267
XXXI.	Character	283
XXXII.	Vice	292
XXXIII.	Poverty	298
XXXIV.	Ability and Opportunity	304
XXXV.	Beauty	314
XXXVI.	Love	321
XXXVII.	Courtship	328
XXXVIII.	Marriage	337
XXXIX.	After Marriage	348
XL.	Advantages of Wedlock	364
XLI.	Tell Your Wife	372
XLII.	Courtesy	375
XLIII.	Home Government	379
XLIV.	Broken Ties	388
XLV.	Brevity of Life	391
XLVI.	The Silent Shore	396

Between two worlds life hovers, like a star
'Twixt night and morn upon the horizon's verge.
How little do we know that which we are!
How less what we may be! The eternal surge
Of time and tide rolls on, and bears afar
Our bubbles; as the old burst new emerge,
Lashed from the foam of ages, while the graves
Of empires heave but like some passing waves.
—Byron.

THE VOYAGE OF LIFE.

I.

THE VOYAGE OF LIFE.

LIFE is the spring-time of eternity—a voyage to the grave. The sea we have to navigate, viewed in prospect, looks smooth and inviting; but beneath, it conceals shoals, quick sands, and rocks; and great multitudes in attempting to reach the distant shores are shipwrecked and lost. No man knows his destiny. We pass our lives in regretting the past, complaining of the present, and indulging false hopes of the future. Every anniversary of a birth-day is the dispelling of a dream. We aspire and aspire and then give in. Life in this particular is like a coffin, which widens up to a certain point, and then tapers off again. Happy the man who sees a God employed in all the good and ill that chequer life.

Life bears us on like the stream of a mighty river. Our boat at first glides down the narrow channel, through the playful murmurings of the little brook and the windings of its grassy borders. The trees shed their blossoms over our young heads; the flowers seem to offer themselves to our young hands; we are happy in hope, and grasp eagerly at the beauties around us, but the stream hurries us on, and still our hands are empty. Our course in youth and manhood is along a deeper and wider channel, among objects more striking and magnificent. We are animated at the moving pictures and enjoyment and industry all around us; we are excited at some short-lived disappointment. The stream bears us on, and our joys and griefs are alike behind us. We may be shipwrecked, but we cannot be delayed. Whether rough or smooth, the river hastens on until the roar of the ocean is in our ears and the tossing of the waves is beneath our feet, and the floods are lifted up around us, and we take leave of earth and its inhabitants, until of our future voyage there is no witness save the Infinite and Eternal.

The great art and philosophy of life is to make

the best of the present, whether it be good or bad; and to bear the one with resignation and patience, and to enjoy the other with thankfulness and moderation. Are we brought into the world, and allowed to occupy a place in it, only that we may pursue trifles! that we may brutishly gratify our appetites and passions! that we may leave the world at last, perhaps at the expiration of three score years and ten, without having derived any advantage from being in it, or conferring a single benefit upon it! Memory goes like a resurrectionist to the graves of our past errors and crimes, and shows us their skeletons. The conventional robes in which we dressed them to make them seemly are gone—the tinsel of subterfuge and sophistry with which we bedecked their loathsomeness has fallen away—self-deception is no longer possible, and we shrink from the foul offspring of our misguided souls, but cannot, dare not repudiate them. If the young doubt the resemblance of this picture, let them ask the old, and they will learn that its drawing is correct and its tints true. Ah, if the man of the world were only as careful to consult his conscience on points of moral right, as to consult his lawyer on points of law, how much misery would he not escape both in his life of action and his life of afterthought.

We have often been impressed by the deep significance of the phrase which Dickens has given as a title to one of his Christmas stories, " The Battle of Life." It is full of solemn meanings. All our hours, from the cradle to the grave, are but a series of antagonisms. Hunger, fatigue, sickness, temptation, sin, remorse, sorrow—these are the strong powers with which we must wage continual war. Foes beset us from without and from within, and make life one long and earnest battle. But there are victories to be won on the field, more glorious than those which crimsoned Marathon and Waterloo. Evil habits may be subdued— fiery passions brought under the control of principle — temptations resisted — self-denial cheerfully sustained, and life itself consecrated to high and holy purposes. To triumph over the infirmities of a perverted nature, and render life, once deformed by passion and stained by sin, beautiful with love made manifest in deeds of beneficence, is worthier our ambition than all the blood-wrought heroism that ever linked a name to a world's remembrance. Every day witnesseth triumphs such as these —yet fame proclaims them not. What matters it? In the serene depths of these all conquering spirits, God's peace abides, and harmonies are heard, such as the angels make, when they welcome the victorious soul from the conflicts of this, to the raptures of the heavenly world.

We have been watching with intense interest, a man's journey up the roof of yonder building. It may be some sixty feet to the top, and his only foothold and dependence is a frail ladder, that shakes with his every step. It is a fearful thing to hang thus suspended—one round loosened, his hold is lost, and death is certain. We are all going up the steep ladder of life, and we are not so sure as he that the round before us is not loose. Let us take heed —like him, be slow and sure; like him feel that we hang midway between earth and the grave; like him hold closely on to the sides, God's providences, and as he at lasts mounts to the top, there to rest from his labors, so shall we attain to Heaven, not like him for a transient hour, but a whole and delightful eternity.

That state is capable of the greatest enjoyment where necessity urges, but not painfully; where effort is required, but as much as possible without anxiety; where the spring and summer of life are preparatory to the harvest of autumn and the repose of winter. Then is every season sweet, and in a well spent life, the last the best—the season of calm enjoyment the richest in recollections, the brightest in hope. Good training and a fair start constitute a more desirable patrimony than wealth; and those parents who study their children's welfare rather than the gratification of their own avarice or vanity, would do well to think of this. Is it better to run a successful race, or to begin and end at the goal? Life has an ultimate purpose. We are not appointed to pass through this life, barely that we may live. We are not impelled, both by disposition and necessity, to buy and sell, barely that we may get it. There is an end in business beyond supply. There is an object in the acquisition of wealth beyond success. There is a final cause of human traffic; and that is VIRTUE!

The laugh of mirth which vibrates through

the heart; the tears which freshen the dry wastes within; the music which brings childhood back; the prayer that calls the future near; the doubt which makes us meditate; the death which startles us with mystery; the hardships that force us to struggle; the anxiety that ends in trust—these are the true nourishments of our natural being.

Life is no speculative adventure with those who feel its value and duties. It has a deeper purpose, and its path becomes distinct and easy in proportion as it is earnestly and faithfully pursued. The rudest or the most refined pursuit, if adapted to the wants and capacities of the pursuer, has a truth, a beauty, and a satisfaction. All ships on the ocean are not steamers or packets, but all freight bearers, fitted to their tasks; and the smallest shallop nobly fulfills its mission, while it pushes on toward its destined port, nor shifts its course because ships career to other points of the compass. Let man ride himself on the ocean of Time. Let him learn by nature whether he is a shallop or a ship, a coaster or an ocean steamer; and then freighting himself according to his capacity and the market he should seek, fling his sail to the breeze, riding with wind and tide, if they go his course, but beating resolutely against them if they cross his path.

Almost every man wastes part of his life in attempts to display qualities which he does not possess, and to gain applause which he cannot keep. We often speak of being "settled in life." We might as well speak of anchoring in the midst of the Atlantic Ocean. Like the leaf, life has its fading. We speak and think of it with sadness, just as we think of the Autumn season. But there should be no sadness at the fading of a life that has done well its work. If we rejoice at the advent of a new life, if we welcome the coming of a new pilgrim to the uncertainties of this world's way, why should there be so much gloom when all these uncertainties are passed, and life at its waning wears the glory of a competent task? Beautiful as is childhood in its freshness and innocence, its beauty is that of untried life. It is the beauty of promise, of Spring, of the bud. A holier and rarer beauty is the beauty which the waning life of faith and duty wears. It is the beauty of a thing completed; and as men come together to congratulate each other when some great work has been achieved, and see in its concluding nothing but gladness, so ought we to feel when the setting sun flings back its beams upon a life that has answered well life's purpose. When the bud drops blighted, and the mildew blasts the early grain, and there goes all hope of the harvest, one may well be sad; but when the ripened year sinks amid its garniture of Autumn flowers and leaves, why should we regret or murmur? And so a life that is ready and waiting for the " well done " of God, whose latest virtues and charities are the noblest, should be given back to God in uncomplaining reverence, we rejoicing that the earth is capable of so much goodness, and is permitted such virtue. Like flakes of snow that fall unperceived upon the earth, the seemingly unimportant events of life succeed one another. Thus imperceptibly and swiftly life passes away. Life's moments are ever fleeting; the generations of men come and pass away like the leaves of the forest: as the year blooms and fades, so does human life.

Men seldom think of the great event of

death until the shadows fall across their own path, hiding forever from their eyes the traces of loved ones whose living smiles were the sunlight of their existence. Death is the great antagonist of life, and the cold thought of the tomb is the skeleton of all feasts. We do not want to go through the dark valley, although its passage may lead to paradise; and with Charles Lamb, we do not want to lie down in the muddy grave, even with kings and princes for our bed-fellows. But the fiat of nature is inexorable, there is no appeal from the great law which dooms us to dust. We flourish and we fade as the leaves of the forest; and the flowers that bloom and wither in a day have not a frailer hope upon life than the mightiest monarch that ever shook the earth with his footsteps. Generations of men appear and vanish as the grass, and the countless multitude which fills the world to-day, will to-morrow disappear as the footsteps on the shore. This is life. If we die to-day, the sun will shine as brightly and the birds sing as sweetly to-morrow. Business will not be suspended a moment, and the great mass will not bestow a thought upon our memories. Is he dead? will be the solemn inquiry of a few as they pass to their work. But no one will miss us except our immediate connections, and in a short time they will forget us, and laugh as merrily as when we sat beside them. Thus shall we all, now active in life, pass away. Our children crowd close behind us, and they will soon be gone. In a few years not a living being can say, "I remember him! We lived in another age, and have no business with those who slumber in the tomb." This is life; how rapidly it passes!

> "So live, that when thy summons comes to join
>   The innumerable caravan, which moves
>   To that mysterious realm where each shall take
>   His chamber in the silent halls of death,
>   Thou go, not like the quarry-slave at night
>   Scourged to his dungeon; but sustained and soothed
>   By an unfaltering trust, approach thy grave
>   Like one who wraps the drapery of his couch
>   About him, and lies down to pleasant dreams."

II.

INFANCY.

A BABE in a house is a well-spring of pleasure, a messenger of peace and love, a resting-place for innocence on earth; a link between angels and men.

A babe is a mother's anchor, she cannot go far from her moorings. And yet a true mother never lives so little in the present as when by the side of the cradle. Her thoughts follow the imagined future of her child. That babe is the boldest of pilots, and guides her fearless thoughts down through scenes of coming years. The old ark never made such a voyage as the cradle daily makes. Maternity is the perfecting, not only of womanhood, but humanity. And to the *first baby*, has God given the sacred power to complete the circle of human sympathies, to waken the conscious solidarity of human interests. Every mother that *is* a mother, pictures the whole troop of loves, joys, and sorrows hovering around "the first baby." She lays every mother's baby in the cradle which held her own first baby, and listens to the songs that gush forth, or as they are softly murmured in the mother-heart. To a mother's heart, every mother's baby is the representative of inestimable treasure; it is an estate held in "fee simple;" a little sub-soiler that leaves no affections fallow, no sympathies isolated from the claims of a common humanity.

Welcome to the parents the puny struggler, strong in his weakness, his little arms more irresistible than the soldier's, his lips touched with persuasion which Chatham and Pericles in manhood had not. His unaffected lamentations when he lifts up his voice on high; or, more beautiful, the sobbing child—the face all liquid grief, as he tries to swallow his vexation—soften all hearts to pity, and to mirthful and clamorous compassion. The small despot asks so little that all reason and all nature are on his side. His ignorance is more charming than all knowledge, and his little sins more bewitching than any virtue. His flesh is angel's flesh, all alive. "Infancy," said Coleridge, "presents body and spirit in unity; the body is all animated." All day, between his three or four sleeps, he coos like a pigeon house, sputters and spurs, and puts on his faces of importance, and when he fasts, the little Pharisee fails not to sound his trumpet before him. By lamplight, he delights in shadows on the wall; by daylight, in yellow and scarlet. Carry him out of doors—he is overpowered by the light and by the extent of natural objects, and is silent.

The first baby!—why, it brings treasures with it! True, its little hand is empty; but then it brings to light and activity unrevealed capacities, looses the sealed fountains, and assays the unwrought treasure of the human soul. It is not *all* joy—that baby gift;—if it were it could not be a joy forever. It is not all *sorrow;* if it were, the fountains of the heart it stirs, could not grow pure to reflect the heaven above; would not flow down the stream of time, bearing rich freight for unknown and unborn posterity. But see, it lays its tiny hand on the heart, and it forgets to beat for self. It pillows its soft cheek on the bosom that, hitherto, had looked out upon the struggling world—all unlinked to its wants, all unmoved by its destiny—and henceforth that bosom is the asylum of the orphan, the refuge of the oppressed, the sanctuary which invites a world lying in wretchedness to the banquet of love, to the smiles of a common Father. And why?—Ah, that baby is the medium through which the helplessness, the wants and the promise of humanity have appealed to the *woman*. In behalf of the *race*, it has whispered *mother!* and looking into its trusting, worshipping eyes, she accepts the consecration, answers the appeal with a deep, an eternity echoed—my *child*.

No one feels the death of a child as a mother feels it. The father cannot feel it thus. True, there is a vacancy in his home and a heaviness in his heart. There is a chain of association that at set times comes round with a broken link—there are memories of endearment, a keen sense of loss, a weeping over crushed hopes, and a pain of wounded affection. But the mother feels that one has been taken away who was still closer to her heart. Hers has been the office of constant ministration. Every graduation of feature developed before her eyes; she detected every new gleam of infant intelligence; she heard the first utterance of every stammering word; she was the refuge of its fears, the supply of its wants; and every task of affection wove a new link, and made dear to her its object. And when her child dies, a portion of her own life as it were dies with it. How can she give her darling up, with all these living memories, these fond associations? The timid hands that have so often taken in trust and love, how can she fold them on its sinless breast, and surrender them to Death? The feet whose wanderings she watched so narrowly, how can she see them straightened to go down into the dark valley? The head that she had pressed to her lips and bosom, that she has watched in peaceful slumber and in burning sickness, a hair of which she could not see harmed, oh, *how* can she consign it to the dark chamber of the grave? It was a gleam of sunshine and a voice of perpetual gladness in her home; she had learned from it blessed lessons of simplicity, sincerity, purity, faith; it had unsealed within her a gushing, never-ebbing tide of affection; when suddenly it was taken away, and that home is left dark and silent; and to the vain and heart-rending aspiration, " Shall that dear child never return again?" there breaks in response, through the cold gray silence, " Nevermore—oh, nevermore!" The heart is like a forsaken mansion, and that word goes echoing through its desolate chambers. And yet, fond mother! ("Time brings such wonderous easing,") thou wilt in after years look back, with a not unpleasing sadness, even upon this scene of grief:

EMPTY CRADLES.

Mrs. Georgie A. H. McLeod.

Oh, the empty, empty cradles,
   That must now be put away,
For the little ones will need them
   Never more by night or day,
For the pure and dreamless sleepers,
   Never more they'll rock to rest,
Their bright heads upon the pillows,
   Shall no more be softly prest!

In the still and solemn nightfall,
   Death's pale angel noiseless sped,
"I have gathered only Lilies,
   For my Lord, to-day," he said;

Oh, the Lilies, the White Lilies,
    That made earthly homes so bright,
How many, many buds are missing,
    Since the happy morning light!

Waxen hands, with blossoms in them,
    Faces very white and fair,
Curtained eyes, like hidden star-light,
    Silken rings of sunny hair.
Hushed and still, we gaze upon them
    And we scarcely know our loss;
But to-morrow we shall feel it,
    Almost crushed beneath the cross.

Little robes, so richly broidered,
    Wrought with so much love and pride
Dainty laces, pale, pure ribbons,
    They must all be laid aside;
For in glorious robes of brightness
    Are the little ones arrayed,
All unstained by earth the whiteness,
    Such a little while they stayed.

Ah, the busy, busy mornings,
    And the nights of anxious care;
Now, there is no need of watching,
    There'll be time enough to spare.
There's no baby's voice, we'll listen,
    Thinking that we hear it oft;
On our face no baby fingers,
    Touches like the rose leaves soft.

INFANCY.

Never mind the noisy household,
  Nor loud foot-falls on the stair,
'Twill not wake the peaceful sleeper,
  There's no baby anywhere.
In a casket, white as snow-flakes,
  Nestling all among the flowers,
Are the pure and stainless Lilies,
  That a little while were ours.

In our dreams 'midst dazzling brightness,
  And a rapturous burst of song,
Through our tears, we saw above us,
  Oh! the radiant spirit throng!
In their arms so softly cradled
  Our own little ones we know,
And we hear them whisper gently,
  "The White Lilies from below."

Wide the shining gates are opened,
  For the children are at home,
Back to us, come the sweet echoes,
  "Oh, suffer them to come!"
Put away the empty cradles,
  Keep we only in our sight
That bright glimpse of the fair dwelling
  Which the children have to-night.

III.

CHILDHOOD.

And say to parents what a holy charge
Is theirs; with what a kingly power their love
Might rule the fountains of the new-born mind.
Warn them to wake at early dawn and sow
Good seed, before the world has sown its tares.

THE child is father of the man. Men are but children of a larger growth. How often do we meet with this array of words! Yet how insensible we are to the profound philosophy they enwrap. See yonder group of children now playing together —like birds among the blossoms of earth, haunting all the green shadowy places, and rejoicing in the bright air; happy and beautiful faces, and as changeable as happy, with eyes brimful of joy, and with hearts playing upon their little faces like sunshine upon clear waters; among those who are now idling together on that slope, or hunting butterflies together on the edge of that wood,—you see our future men and women, not only the gifted and the powerful, the wise and the eloquent, the ambitious and the renowned, but the wicked and the treacherous, the abandoned profligate and the faithless husband, the gambler, the drunkard and the robber.

Among them, and that other little troop just appearing, children with yet happier faces and pleasanter eyes, the blossoms of the future— the mothers of nations, the unfaithful wife and the broken-hearted husband, the proud betrayer and his pale victim, the living and breathing portents and prodigies, the embodied virtues and vices, of another age and of another world. If this picture be true, parents, what a responsible charge you have. To you are entrusted these beautiful gems of God, and He will hold you responsible for their proper culture. Upon your training will rest their future destiny and a nation's hope. How important then that parents should remember the words of Archbishop Leighton, who says, "Fill the bushel with good wheat, and there will be no room for chaff and rubbish." This is a good thought for every mother while tending her children, and watching the growth of their power in body and mind.

"As soon as they be born," the Bible says, "children go astray speaking lies." So soon, therefore, will a Christian mother begin to "train her child in the way he should go," that *good habits* may be formed, ready to carry out *good principles* as the child grows old enough to understand the reason for his conduct.

Not without design has God implanted in the maternal breast that strong love of her children which is felt everywhere. This lays deep and broad the foundation for the child's future education from parental hands. Nor without designs has Christ commanded, "Feed my lambs,"—meaning to inculcate upon his Church the duty of caring for the children of the Church and the world at the earliest possible period. Nor can parents and all well-wishers to humanity be too earnest and careful to fulfill the promptings of their very nature and the command of Christ in this matter. Influence is as quiet and imperceptible on the child's mind as the falling of snow flakes on the meadow. One cannot tell the hour when the human mind is not in condition of receiving impressions from exterior moral forces. In innumerable instances, the most secret and unnoticed influences have been in operation for months and even years to break down the strongest barriers of the human heart, and work out its moral ruin, while yet the fondest parents and friends have been unaware of the working of such unseen agents of evil. Not all at once does any heart become utterly bad. The error is in this : that parents are not conscious how early the seeds of vice are sown and take root. It is as the Gospel declares, "While men slept, the enemy came and sowed tares, and went his way."

Grown persons are apt to put a lower estimate than is just, on the understanding of children. They rate them by what they know; and children know very little; but their comprehension is great. Hence the continual wonder of those who are unaccustomed to them, at the old fashioned ways of some lone little one, who has no play-fellows—and at the odd mixture of the folly and wisdom in its sayings. A continual battle goes on in the child's mind, between what it knows and what it comprehends. Its answers are foolish from partial ignorance; and wise from extreme quickness of apprehension. The great art of education is so to train this last faculty as neither to depress nor over-exert it. The matured mediocrity of many an infant prodigy proves both the degree of expansion in which it is possible to force a child's intellect, and the boundary which nature has set to the success of such false culture.

A majority of character, throughout civilized society, gets its mood and bent from home influences. Education, it has been well said, forms the common mind, and home influences are the most impressive common educators. Good or bad, their potency is the same.

Do not command children under six years of age to keep anything secret, not even the pleasure you may be preparing as a surprise for a dear friend. The cloudless heaven of youthful openheartedness should not be overcast, not even by the rosy dawn of shyness; otherwise, children will soon learn to conceal their own secrets as well as yours.

We desire to enter a protest against the

fashion among many mothers, of referring their children to "father," in matters that require the exercise of judgment and discretion. Of course it is wrong for parents to discuss such matters before their children. What we mean to say is, that the equal sovereignty of parents should be an unquestioned thing in the minds of children. There should be no such thing as an appeal from the decisions of the one to the other with hope of a reversal of judgment. Mothers who evade such duty, not only depreciate their own value in the eyes of their children, but serve to weaken and render valueless the judgment and wisdom of women in general, in the estimation of both their sons and daughters. Women often feel suspicious of the excellence of their own judgment, and are prone to appeal to men for ultimate decisions. In the "long run" of affairs, the judgment of women is really superior to that of men. The difference lies in the conscience and the decisive qualities. In the management and training of children, a faulty decision now and then, is not so fatal in result, as a continually wavering and negative manner. Do not infer from this, that all matters pertaining to children should be decided at once, and never deviated from. There are many times when a child should be allowed to plead his own cause, and parents can never be too sympathetic with their children. A lack of it constitutes the direct griefs of childhood.

A sagacious observer says :—" When I see children going to their father for comfort, I am sure there is something wrong with their mother."

Do not make too much of their mistakes and faults. How can one be a child and not be full of faults? Explain their mistakes gently. Be patient! Wait for them! Children must have time to grow. Somebody had to wait for you. Never let fear make a gulf between the child and you. Within due bounds liberty is the best thing for a child, as it is for a man. It will lead to irregularities, but out of these will come experience, and, gradually, self-control. The object of all family government is to teach children to get along without being governed. They must therefore be trusted; even if they abuse it, they must be trusted. Keep them busy with pleasant work, if possible. Awaken in them curiosity about the

things which lie around them. A very little instruction will make children curious of plants, minerals, natural history, of literary curiosities, autographs, postage-stamp collections, and a thousand things which will inspire pleasure in their reason rather than in their appetites.

Do unto children, always, even as ye, when ye were children, would have been done by. Thus, reader, shall you enlarge and soften many an intellect and heart; thus prevent many a home being made sad and desolate by domestic bitterness.

Everybody's rights seem to be recognized and talked about but the children's; and yet we venture to say that those of none are infringed upon more than theirs. We who are not so far removed from childhood, either in accumulation of years or lack of sympathy, can remember how many childish grievances we had—how dreadful they seemed to us then, and of how little importance the rules sometimes have seemed since we looked back with older eyes. It is well to look at these things in our dealings with our children, who are governed and scolded and found fault with far too much. Dr. Hall, in his excellent work of

"Health by Good Living," gives parents a good piece of advice in telling them to let the children alone when they gather around the family table. It is a cruelty to hamper them with manifold rules and regulations about this, and that, and the other. As long as their conduct is harmless as to others, encourage them in their cheeriness. Suppose a child does not sit as straight as a ramrod at the table; suppose a cup or tumbler slips through his little fingers and deluges the plate of food below, and the goblet is smashed, and the table-cloth is ruined; do not look a thousand scowls and thunders, and scare the poor thing to the balance of its death, for it was scared half to death before; it "did not go to do it." Did you never let a glass slip through your fingers since you were grown? Instead of sending the child away from the table in anger, if not even with a threat for this or any other little nothing, be as generous as you would to an equal or superior guest to whom you would, with a more or less obsequious smile, " it is of no possible consequence." That would be the form of expression even to a stranger guest, and yet to your own child you remorselessly, and revengefully, and angrily mete out a swift punishment, which for the time almost breaks its heart, and belittles you amazingly. The proper and more enlightened mode of dealing out reproof to the child, when it seems necessary, is to take no notice of mishaps or bad behavior at the time, or to go further, and divert attention from them at the very instant, if possible, or to make a kind apology for them; but afterwards, in an hour or two, or better still, next day, draw the child's attention to the fault, if fault it is, in a friendly and loving manner; point out the impropriety in some kindly way; show where it was wrong or rude, and appeal to the child's self-respect or manliness. This is the best way to correct all family errors. Sometimes it may not succeed; sometimes harsh measures may be required; but try the deprecating or the kindly method with equanimity of mind, and failure will be of rare occurrence. Never mar home life by cross words or peevishness.

This world is full of rough places, and its jagged features are as frequently seen in the faces around us, as in its rocks and caverns. The father, stern and unyielding, drives sunshine from the house, or the mother, full of responsibility, cuffs the children into corners, and has order and neatness at the expense of their liberty and happiness. Perhaps a youth of seventeen presumes to govern, and ma and children must keep still. The novel-reading young lady becomes horribly nervous if the little ones touch the sofa on which she reclines. The girl in the kitchen frowns them out of her presence, or scolds them, without shame. Poor little things! how much they seem to be in the way. One moment petted and carried in our bosoms, the next cuffed and abused as if the cause of all our trials. A disagreement between parents is frequently revenged upon the children, and every careless act is laid to their charge. A lost spoon, a broken china, a misplaced book, is referred to them, and before they can command language to defend themselves, they take it for granted that pa, ma, big brother and sister must be right and they wrong. Where is the wisdom in saying to a child, be a man? If the mind be curbed and humbled too much in children—if their spirits be abased and broken by too strict a hand over them—they lose all their vigor and industry.

Make room for children. Room and freedom for them at home, that they may expand and strengthen those faculties and functions which are soon to constitute the man-and-womanhood of a generation. Room for them in the nursery and on the play-ground, with opportunity and freedom to exercise, if you would have them hearty, cheerful, and home-loving. Too much, in the main, are children burrowed and quashed at home, where they should be encouraged to gambol and rejoice—at home, where their voices should ring out merry as the voices of summer birds. Room for the children at school. At school, where they are too often imprisoned, stifled, and dwarfed in body and mind. Room and freedom for the children at school, that they may breathe fresh air and commune with their teachers, not as masters—stern, unbending and unsympathising—but as intellectual guides and social friends. Room for the children at church, too, and see that they are *attracted*—as they can be—thither, and not driven with the "rod of correction," or the chilling rebuke. More room, greater care for, and a higher common estimate of children, if you would stimulate their ambition to win your regard. Children are generally older, more observing, and more capable than they seem. The less you ignore them, the less will they ignore you. The more you cultivate them, the more will they cultivate you. Give them no room, teach them to think you believe them nobodies, and ten to one they will strive to justify such a belief. Room for the children, God's holiest and tenderest blessing—the light of our homes and the delight of our hearts. Room for them everywhere, and not least in the public place, the public conveyance, at the public table. Tuck them not in a corner, crowd them not to the wall, leave them not forever to the second course and the fragments of the feast, unless you would have them grow up thoughtless of justice and selfish as yourselves, to practice, in turn upon their children as you practice upon them.

IV.

THE RIGHTS OF CHILDREN.

BABY has a right, too frequently denied it, *to be let alone.* It ought to be a rule in the nursery never to disturb the infant when it is happy and quiet. Older children, too, two, three, and four years of age, who are amusing themselves in a peaceful, contented way, ought not to be wantonly interfered with. I have often seen a little creature lying in its crib cooing, laughing, crooning to itself in the sweetest baby fashion, without a care in the world to vex its composure, when in would come mamma or nurse, seize it, cover it with endearments, and effectually break up its tranquility. Then, the next time, when these thoughtless people wanted it to be quiet, they were surprised that it refused to be so. It is habit and training which makes little children restless and

fretful, rather than natural disposition, in a multitude of cases. A healthy babe, coolly and loosely dressed, judiciously fed, and frequently bathed, will be good and comfortable if it have not too much attention. But when it is liable a dozen times a day to be caught wildly up, bounced and jumped about, smothered with kisses, poked by facetious fingers, and petted till it is thoroughly out of sorts, what can be expected of it? How would fathers and mothers endure the martyrdom to which they allow the babies to be subjected?

Another right which every baby has is to its own mother's care and supervision. The mother may not be strong enough to hold her child and carry it about, to go with it on its outings, and to personally attend to all its wants. Very often it is really better for both mother and child that the strong arms of an able-bodied woman should bear it through its months of helplessness. Still, no matter how apparently worthy of trust a nurse or servant may be, unless she have been tried and proved by long and faithful service and friendship, a babe is too precious to be given unreservedly to her care. The mother herself, or an elder sister or auntie, should hover protectingly near the tiny creature, whose life-long happiness may depend on the way its babyhood is passed. Who has not seen in the city parks the beautifully-dressed infants, darlings evidently of homes of wealth and refinement, left to bear the beams of the sun and stings of gnats and flies, while the nurses gossipped together, oblivious of the flight of time? Mothers are often quick to resent stories of the neglect or cruelty of their employees, and cannot be made to believe that their own children are sufferers. And the children are too young to speak.

The lover of little ones can almost always see the subtle difference which exists between the babies whom mothers care for, and the babies who are left to hirelings. The former have a sweeter, shyer, gladder look than the latter. Perhaps the babies who are born, so to speak, with silver spoons in their mouths, are better off than those who came to the heritage of a gold spoon. The gold-spooners have lovely cradles and vassinets. They wear Valenciennes lace and embroidery, and fashion dictates the cut of their bibs, and the length of their flowing robes. They are waited upon by bonnes in picturesque aprons and caps, and the doctor is sent for whenever they have the colic. The little silver-spooners, on the other hand, are arrayed in simple slips, which the mother made herself in dear, delicious hours, the sweetest in their mystic joy which happy womanhood knows. They lie on the sofa, or on two chairs with a pillow placed carefully to hold them, while she sings at her work, spreads the snowy linen on the grass, moulds the bread, and shells the peas. The mother's hands wash and dress them, the father rocks them to sleep, the proud brothers and sisters carry them to walk, or wheel their little wagons along the pavement. Fortunate babies of the silver spoon!

Alas and alack! for the babies who have never a spoon at all, not even a horn or a leaden one. Their poor parents love them, amid the squalid circumstances which hem them in, but they can do little for their well-being, and they die by hundreds in garrets and cellars and close tenement rooms. When the rich and charitable shall devise some way to care for the babies of the poor, we shall have taken a long step forward in the direction of social and moral elevation.

Children also have a right to ask questions and to be fairly answered; not to be snubbed as if they were guilty of an impertinence, nor ignored as though their desire for information were of no consequence, nor misled as if it did not signify whether true or false impressions were made upon their minds.

The child has a right to his individuality, to be himself and no other; to maintain against the world the divine fact for which he stands. And before this fact father, mother, instructor should stand reverently; seeking rather to understand and interpret its significance than to wrest it from its original purpose. It is not necessarily to be inscribed with the family name, nor written over with family traditions. Nature delights in surprise and will not guarantee that the children of her poets shall sing, nor that every Quaker baby shall take kindly to drab color, or have an inherent longing for a scoop-bonnet or a broad-brimmed hat.

In the very naming of a child his individuality should be recognized. He should not be invested with the cast-off cognomen of some dead ancestor or historical celebrity, a name musty as the grave-clothes of the original wearer—dolefully redolent of old associations—a ghostly index-finger forever pointing to the past. Let it be something fresh; a new name standing for a new fact, the suggestion of a history yet to be written, a prophecy to be fulfilled. The ass was well enough clothed in his own russet; but when he would put on the skin of the lion, every attribute became contemptible. Commonplace people slip easily through the world; but when we would find them heralded by great names, we resent the incongruity, and insist upon making them less than they are. George Washington selling peanuts, Julius Cæsar as a bootblack, and Virgil a vender of old clothes, make but a sorry figure.

We are indebted to our children for constant incentives to noble living; for the perpetual reminder that we do not live to ourselves alone; for their sakes we are admonished to put from us the debasing appetite, the unworthy impulse; to gather into our lives every noble and heroic quality, every tender and attractive grace.

We owe them gratitude for the dark hours which their presence has brightened, for the helplessness and dependence which have won us from ourselves; for the faith and trust which it is evermore their mission to renew; for their kisses on cheeks wet with tears, and on brows that but for that caressing had furrowed into frowns.

Can torture chamber be more dreadful than the juvenile party, the necessary parade of the Christmas-dinner, to a shy boy? I have sometimes taken the hand of such a one, and have found it cold and clammy; desperate was the struggle of that young soul, afraid of he knew not what, caught by the machinery of society, which mangled him at every point, crushed every nerve, and filled him with faintness and fear. How happy he might have been with that brood of young puppies in the barn, or the soft rabbits in their nest of hay! How grand he was, paddling his poor leaky boat down the rapids, jumping into the river, and dragging it with his splendid strength over the rocks! Nature and he were friends; he was not afraid of her; she recognized her child and greeted him with smiles. The young animals loved him, and his dog looked up into his fair blue eyes, and recognized his king. But this creature must be tamed; he must be brought into prim parlors, and dine with propriety; he must dress himself in garments which scratch, and pull, and hurt him; boots must be put on his feet which pinch; he must be clean,—terrible injustice to a faun who loves to roll down-hill, to grub for roots, to follow young squirrels to their lair, and to polish old guns rather than his manner.

And then the sensitive boy, who has a finer grain than the majority of his fellows, suddenly thrown into the pandemonium of a public school! Nails driven into the flesh could not inflict such pain as such a one suffers; and the scars remain. One gentleman told me, in mature life, that the loss of a toy stolen from him in childhood still rankled. How much of the infirmity of human character may be traced to the anger, the sense of wounded feeling, engendered by a wrong done in childhood when one is helpless to avenge!

All this may be called the necessary hardening process, but I do not believe in it. We have learned how to temper iron and steel, but we have not learned how to treat children. Could it be made a money-making process, like the Bessemer, I believe one could learn how to temper the human character. Our instincts of intense love for our children are not enough; we should study it as a science. The human race is very busy; it has to take care of itself, and to feed its young; it must conquer the earth — perhaps it has not time to study Jim and Jack and Charley, and Mary and Emily and Jane, as problems. But, if it had, would it not perhaps pay? There would be fewer criminals.

Many observers recommend a wise neglect —not too much inquiry, but a judicious surrounding of the best influences, and then let your young plant grow up. Yes; but it should be a very wise neglect—it should be a neglect which is always on the watch lest some insidious parasite, some unnoticed but strong bias of character, take possession of the child and mould or ruin him. Of the ten boys running up yonder hill, five will be failures, two will be moderate successes, two will do better, one will be great, good, and distinguished. If such are the terrible statistics— and I am told that they are so—who is to blame? Certainly the parent or guardian, or circumstances—and what is circumstance?

V.

BOYS.

THE boy is an offense in himself. He must have something to do, and as his hands are idle the proverbial provider of occupation for idle hands is always ready with instructions for him. A boy makes noise in utter defiance of the laws of acoustics. Shoe him in velvet, and carpet your house as you will, your boy shall make such a hubbub with his heels as no watchman's rattle ever gave forth. Doors in his hands always shut with a violence which jars the whole house, and he is certain to acquire each day the art of screaming or whistling in some wholly new and excruciating way. Loving his mother so violently that his caresses derange her attire and seriously endanger her bones, ready to die in her defense if need be, he nevertheless torments her from morning to night, and allows

her no possible peace until slumber closes his throat and eyelids, and deprives his hands and feet of their demoniac cunning.

In public your boy is equally a nuisance. Collectively or individually he offends the public in the streets. Whatever he does is sure to be wrong. He monopolizes space and takes to himself all the air there is for acoustical purposes. Your personal peculiarities interest him, and with all the frankness of his soul he comments upon your appearance, addressing his remarks to his fellow on the next block.

Nevertheless the boy has his uses. He is the material out of which men are to be made for the next generation. He is not a bad fellow,—that is to say, he is not intentionally or consciously bad. There are springs in his limbs which keep him in perpetual motion, and the devil of uproar of which he is possessed utters the ear-piercing sounds which annoy his elders, but the utterances of which he can no more restrain than he can keep his boots or trousers from wearing out. In a ten-acre lot, well away from the house, the boy is a picturesque and agreeable person ; it is only when one must come into closer contact with him that his presence causes suffering and suggests a statue to King Herod. It is in cities that the boy makes himself felt most disagreeably, and we fancy the fault is not altogether his. As the steam which bursts boilers would be a perfectly harmless vapor but for the sharp restraint that is put upon it, so the effervescent boy becomes dangerous to social order only when he is confined, when an effort is made to compress him into smaller space than the law of his expansive being absolutely requires. We send him upon the war-path by encroaching upon his hunting-grounds; we drive him into hostility by treating him as a public enemy. In most of our dealings with him in cities, our effort is to suppress him, and it is an unwise system. If his ball-playing in the streets becomes an annoyance, we simply forbid ball-playing in the streets, and it is an inevitable consequence that, deprived of his ball, he will throw stones at street lamps or at policemen, what else is he to do?

The beau ideal of boyhood is somewhere between eight and twelve—though it exists before and after that age—but when within those years, it is invested with its greatest charm. Then is the first spring of intelligence, when all that meets the eye and the ear creates its due wonder. Then the feelings are tender, and there is yet just so much sweet natural helplessness as serves to keep ever warm and active our affection, by demand upon our care, and to engender a reliance upon us, the source of mutual delight.

Boys are gregarious creatures, and when in troops, having confidence in themselves and in each other, they are all noise and sport.

> "Turning to mirth all things of earth,
> As only boyhood can."

But when quite alone, even in their most delightful idleness, sauntering and loitering, by green lanes, or village highways, they show no signs of mirth. Watch them unseen, and you will find the lips apart, the eye inquiring; there is then a look that might be mistaken for pensive, but it is not that, nor is it easy to define; it is, however, singularly expressive of happiness, the result of sensibility and intuitive perception.

What shall we do with boys? What shall

parents do who live in towns and cities? What shall professional men do whose children cannot participate in their parent's work? Instead of keeping them anxiously within doors, thrust them out as much as possible. Do not let watching become spying. Let them have sports and companions, and unwatched liberty. Put them upon their honor. Boys will early respond to this.

The resources of childhood are nearly inexhaustible. Nobody else on this planet is so ingenious in inventing fun as a rollicking boy. His resources in this respect are as original as inexhaustible. In coming down street the other day we had an illustration. A boy of ten years was walking before us with legs that would comport with the body of Daniel Lambert. We looked at him in amazement. "Son, what is the matter with your legs?" "Nothing. My legs are bunkum. Just see 'em walk." And he waddled off like a duck. "What distends your breeches so?" "Sand, sir," said he, with a hearty laugh. True enough, the boy had tied his pants with strings at the bottom, as is done in deep snow, and filled them to the waist with sand. We walked away ruminating upon the vast resources of boyhood to inaugurate a little fun. Happy boyhood! It's a pity that adult life cannot command as much philosophy.

A boy not fond of fun and frolic may possibly make a tolerable man, but he is an intolerable boy.

A boy may be spoiled about as easily as a girl, by injudicious training; no, we will take that back—much easier. In the first place, then, by leading him to depend upon his sisters. Who has not seen the spoiled boy in the man who could not tie his dickey without calling his wife from the breakfast table to help him; or put on his coat without she held the sleeves; or get a drop of hot water when the kettle was right before him? Another way to spoil a boy is to pick up after him. Now that's a thing we wouldn't do (begging pardon of the gentleman) for the President. We hold that there is as much need of neat habits in a boy, as in the gentler sex; and this idea of gathering the coat from the sofa, the vest from the rocking-chair, the boots from the hearth-rug, the collar from under the table, and the neck-cloth from nobody knows where—is perfectly and superlatively ridiculous. Again, why is the boy allowed to use coarse, indelicate expressions, that, from the lips of a girl would call forth well-merited rebuke? Should the mind of the man be made of coarse material because he is expected to jostle his way through the rude elements of human nature? That is not the law of the machinist who controls dumb matter. Though one engine may be ponderous and massive, destined for the roughest work, and another delicate and complicated, there is the same smoothness of material in both—the same polish, the same nice finish. A boy will most surely be spoiled if led to think he can commit offences against morals, which by the parents are considered only masculine—not criminal. Another wrong thing is to bring a boy up for a profession, will he, nill he. Some parents have a respectable horror for dirt, and cannot think of soiled hands and a trade with any degree of complacency. Therefore the world is burdened with burdens to themselves, in the shape of lawyers, doctors, etc., who are too poor to live, and too poor to die—in comfort. Finally, the surest way to spoil a boy is not to instil into his very soul, from the time he is an infant, a true reverence for woman; a regard for her virtue as sacred as the love he bears his mother. Never let her name be trifled with in his presence, or her actions interpreted loosely, else you may hereafter share the disgrace of having given to the world a curse more corrupting than that of all others —a heartless libertine.

My son, are you a sweetener of life? You may disappoint the ambition of your parents, may be unable to distinguish yourself as they fondly hoped, may find your intellectual strength inadequate to your own desires, but let none of these things move you from a determination to be a son of whose moral character they need never be ashamed. Begin early to cultivate a habit of thoughtfulness and consideration for others, especially for those whom you are commanded to honor. Can you begrudge a few extra steps for the mother who never stopped to number those you demanded during your helpless infancy? Have you the heart to slight her requests, or treat her remarks with indifference, when you cannot begin to measure the patient devotion with which she bore with your peculiarities? Anticipate her wants, invite her confidence, be prompt to offer assistance, express your affections as heartily as you did when a child, that the mother may never grieve in secret for the son she has lost.

You are made to be kind, boys, generous, magnanimous. If there is a boy in school who has a club foot, don't let him know you ever saw it. If there is a poor boy with ragged clothes, don't talk about rags in his hearing. If there is a lame boy, assign him some part of the game which does not require running. If there is a hungry one, give him part of your dinner. If there is a dull one, help him to get his lesson. If there is a bright one, be not envious of him; for if one boy is proud of his talents, and another is envious of them, there are two great wrongs, and no more talent than before. If a larger or stronger boy has injured you, and is sorry for it, forgive him. All the school will show by their countenances how much better it is than to have a great fist.

We love to see boys happy. We well remember our school days—how the joyful

scenes of those golden hours rise before us as we write! After a long, a labored session of school, what is finer for boys than a good frolic on the green grass? See them!—they hop and run, and toss their hats and balls; every bone and cord and muscle of their young and active frames is brought into full and vigorous play. Their minds are unpent as well as their bodies. Let boys have exercise. They must have it, and a good deal too; and they must have the right kind, or they will become sickly and dwarfish, their minds feeble, and their feelings peevish and fretful. The open air, and the more free and pure the better, is important to good exercise to any one, but especially the boys. Otherwise they will be pale and weak, as a plant doomed to the shade. They must have exercise which makes them forget themselves, and all their troubles and tasks, and throws the mind and heart into a glow of life and joy.

Boyhood needs its discipline of care as well as manhood. Young shoulders, however, should not carry the load of old, and grow prematurely bowed. Give the boys something that suits their time of life, though it seem boy's play by their elders. They are just released from the confinement of the winter school and need a pleasant change. The excitement of sugar-making comes just in time, and let the boys have a chance. What gala days these are for them among the maples! How the young blood leaps in their veins and flushes their cheeks while the sap is mounting and running and exhaling its maple odors! Now, too, the calves and lambs and pigs are coming into the world, and how naturally the boys take to them. The barn just now is a good school for first lessons in stock-raising and kindness to animals, and the boys here are their own best teachers. Then they can be fitting up the dove cotes and martin boxes and chicken coops, making nests satisfactory for the setting hens, and getting things ready generally for the new-comers. Boys need only to have the yoke fitted to their years, and they will hardly feel easy without it.

Most boys go through a period when they have great need of patient love at home. They are awkward and clumsy, sometimes strangely willful and perverse, and they are desperately conscious of themselves, and very sensitive to the least word of censure or effort at restraint. Authority frets them. They are leaving childhood, but they have not yet reached the sober good sense of manhood. They are an easy prey to the tempter and the sophist. Perhaps they adopt skeptical views, from sheer desire to prove that they are independent, and can do their own thinking. Now is the mother's hour. Her boy needs her now more than when he lay in his cradle. Her finer insight and serener faith may hold him fast, and prevent his drifting into dangerous courses. At all events, there is very much that only a mother can do for her son, and that a son can receive only from his mother, in the critical period of which we are thinking. It is well for him, if she have kept the freshness and brightness of her youth, so that she can now be his companion and friend as well as instructor.

VI.

GIRLS.

GIRLS, and especially those who are members of large families, have much influence at home, where brothers delight in their sisters, and where parents look fondly down on their dear daughters, and pray that their example may influence the boys for good. Girls have much in their power with regard to those boys; they have it in their power to make them gentler, purer, truer, to give them higher opinions of women; to soften their manners and ways; to tone down rough places, and shape sharp, angular corners.

All this, to be done well, must be done by imperceptibly influencing them, and giving them an example of the gentleness, the purity, the politeness and tenderness we wish them to emulate. When we see boys careless to their

elders, rude in manner and coarse in speech, and we know that they have sisters, we often, and I think with reason, conclude that there must be something wrong, and that the sisters are not trying to make them better boys, but leaving things alone, letting them go their own course. Perhaps their excuse would be that they were too much occupied themselves, and that their own studies and pursuits prevent them from being able to pay much attention to their brothers; and "boys will be boys," you know. By all means let boys be boys. I, for one, regard boys far too highly to wish them to be otherwise; but the roughness, and coarseness, and rudeness, of which I speak, are not necessary ingredients of boyhood; and it is you, their sisters, who must prove that they are not. Interest yourselves in their pursuits, show them, by every means in your power, that you do not consider them and their doings beneath your notice; spare an hour from your practicing, from your drawing, from your languages, for their boating or sports, and don't turn contemptuously away from the books and amusements in which they delight, as if, though good enough for them, they are immeasurably below you. Try this behavior, girls, for a short time; it will not harm you, and will benefit them greatly. You will soon find how a gentle word will turn off a sharp answer; how a grieved look will effectually reprove an unfitting expression; how gratefully a small kindness will be received; and how unbounded will be the power for good you will obtain by a continuance of this conduct.

Equally great will a girl's influence be on her younger sisters, in whose eyes she is the perfection of grace and goodness, in whose thoughts she is ever present. Beautiful, exceedingly beautiful, is the close friendship between an elder and a younger sister; but let the elder beware of the influence she exerts. If she herself be careless, frivolous, undutiful, and irreligious, the child will inevitably be so, unless the fatal influence be counteracted by some other holier one. If she gives sharp answers, or shows but little regard for truth, let her not be astonished if the little one be ill-tempered and untruthful; and sorrowful will be the conviction that she has had not a little to do with making her so.

GIRLS.

In school, too, a girl of determined, resolute character will soon take the lead and acquire a certain influence. School-girls are gregarious, and follow naturally any one who is stronger-minded and more decided. When the influence is exercised to elevate the young minds, and give them higher and noble aspirations, it is a salutary and beneficial effect of school life; but when it is otherwise, it is a very sad one. Two or three older girls in a school, having a noble object in view, steadily endeavoring to do right, acting quietly and without ostentation, but seeking humbly to follow in the footsteps Christ has marked out for us, may do an immense amount of good. " A little leaven leaveneth the whole lump."

> We know not half the power, for good or ill,
>   Our daily lives possess o'er one another;
> A careless word may help a soul to kill,
>   Or by one look we may redeem our brother.
>
> 'Tis not the great things that we do or say,
>   But idle words forgot as soon as spoken;
> And little, thoughtless deeds of every day
>   Are stumbling blocks on which the weak are broken.

VII.

YOUNG MEN.

IT is, without doubt, a very joyous thought to you, that you have become a young man. Manhood has long been the fairy land of your boyhood's reveries. Your full heart swells as you exclaim :

"Time on my brow hath set his seal;
I start to find myself a man."

Your spirits flow in rich currents of feeling, and your lively imagination paints the most inviting pictures of the future. To you, life is as the lovely vale of Arno, with its enchanting scenery of groves and gardens, grottoes, palaces and towers ; its transparent lakes, delicious air, and sunny skies.

That you have reached the period of youth is, therefore, for you, a very *serious* fact, "Great destinies lie shrouded" in your swiftly passing hours. Great responsibilities stand in the passages of every-day life. Great dangers lie hidden in the by-paths of life's great highway; and syrens, whose song is as charming as the voice of Calypso, are there to allure you to destruction. Great uncertainty hangs over your future history. God has given you existence, with full power and opportunity to improve it, and be happy. He has given you equal power to despise the gift, and be wretched. Which will you do, is the grand problem to be solved by your choice and conduct.

As a boy, at home, you have sailed upon the calm waters of a quiet river, in a bark, carefully furnished by a mother's love, and safely guided by a father's skill. Now you are sailing through the winding channels, the rocky straits, the rapid, rushing currents, at the river's mouth, into the great sea of active life. And here, for the first time, you are in *command* of the vessel. On *your* skill and caution depends the safety of the passage. Neglect the rules laid down on the chart of experience by previous navigators, take passion for a pilot, place folly at the helm, and your bark will shortly lie a pitiful wreck on the rocks, or be so damaged as to peril your safety on the coming voyage. But study well the intricacies and dangers of your course, take counsel of experience, let caution be your pilot, and, without doubt, you will escape rock, current, eddy, and whirlpool, and, with streamered masts and big white sail, float gayly forth to dare and conquer the perils of the sea beyond.

The young man, as he passes through life, advances through a long line of tempters ranged on either side of him; and the inevitable effect of yielding is degradation in a greater or less degree. Contact with them tends insensibly to draw away from him some portion of the divine electric element with which his nature is charged; and his only mode of resisting them is to utter and to act out his "No" manfully and resolutely. He must decide at once, not waiting to deliberate and balance reasons; for the youth, like "the woman who deliberates, is lost." Many deliberate, without deciding; but "not to resolve, *is* to resolve." A perfect knowledge of man is in the prayer, "Lead us not into temptation." But temptation will come to try the young man's strength; and once yielded to, the power to resist grows weaker and weaker. Yield once, and a portion of virtue has gone. Resist manfully, and the first decision will give strength for life; repeated, it will become a habit.

Up, then, with a heroic spirit, and gird yourself for mortal conflict with the great Apollyon who bestrides your pathway! If he has subdued thousands, thousands have also subdued him. And you, too, may be his conqueror! Look courageously at the chart of your intended voyage! If, by every sunken rock, and beneath every dashing wave, there lies the wreck of youth who perished untimely, there is also a haven, beyond the sea, into which "*a thousand times ten thousand and thousands of thousands*" have triumphantly entered, in defiance of stormy winds and roaring waves. You may do the same, if you will take timely heed to your ways. Success is before you, if you resolutely and wisely seek it. As says a modern writer, " The seas of human life are wide. Wisdom may suggest the voyage, but it must first look to the condition of the ship, and the nature of the merchandise to exchange. Not every vessel that sails from Tarshish will bring back the gold of Ophir. But shall it therefore rot in the harbor? No! Give its sails to the wind!"

But to wrestle vigorously and successfully with any vicious habit, we must not merely be satisfied with contending on the low ground of wordly prudence, though that is of use, but take stand upon a higher moral elevation. Mechanical aids, such as pledges, may be of service to some, but the great thing is to set up a high standard of thinking and acting, and endeavor to strengthen and purify the principles, as well as to reform the habits. For this purpose a youth must study himself, watch his steps, and compare his thoughts and acts with his rule. The more knowledge of himself he gains, the humbler will he be, and perhaps the less confident in his own strength. But the discipline will be found most valuable which is acquired by resisting small present gratifications to secure a prospective greater and higher one. It is the noblest work in self-education.

To be successful in life, to rise above the common herd of mankind, a young man requires certain elements of character. He must possess Integrity, that he may win public confidence; Intelligence, that he may command respect; Industry, that he may collect honey from the flowers of trade; Economy and frugality, to preserve his gains; Energy, by which to surmount obstacles; and Tact, to enable him to adapt himself to the openings of Providence, and to make him the man for the hour of opportunity. These qualifications are, to success in life, as foundations of jasper to a royal palace. Whoever possesses them cannot be an inferior man. To that man who retains them, life cannot be a failure. Nay, he must rise to social superiority; he must win a commanding influence.

Every period of life has its peculiar temptations and dangers. But were we to specify the period which, of all others, is attended with the greatest peril, and most needs to be watched and guarded, we would fix upon that which elapses from fourteen to twenty-one years of age. This, preeminently, is the forming, fixing period; the spring season of disposition and habit; and it is during this season, more than any other, that the character assumes its permanent shape and color, and the young man is wont to take his course for life and for eternity.

But not to confine our remarks to this particular age, it will not be doubted, that the time, during which we usually denominate one *a young man*, is the most important and perilous period of his whole existence. Then the passions, budding and hastening to ripeness, acquire new vigor, become impatient of restraint, and eager for gratification. Then the imagination, unchecked by experience, and unrestrained by judgment, paints the world in false and fascinating colors, and teaches the young bosom to sigh after its vain and forbidden pleasures. Then springs up in the mind, the restless desire of independence and self-control ;—a disposition to throw off the restraints of paternal counsel and authority, and to think and act for itself. "Then the social impulse is felt, and the young man looks around for companions and friends;" then the calling for life is chosen, the principles of action adopted, habits acquired, and those connections in business and society formed, which usually decide the character, and fix the condition, both for this and the future world.

"It is a great point for young men to begin well; for it is in the beginning of life that that system of conduct is adopted which soon assumes the force of habit. Begin well, and the habit of doing well will become quite as easy as the habit of doing badly. Well begun is half ended, says the proverb; and a good beginning is half the battle. Many promising young men have irretrievably injured themselves by a first false step at the commencement of life; while others of much less promising talents, have succeeded simply by beginning well, and going onward. The good practical beginning is, to a certain extent, a pledge, a promise, and an assurance, of the ultimate prosperous issue. There is many a poor creature, now crawling through life, miserable himself and the cause of sorrow to others, who might have lifted up his head and prospered, if, instead of merely satisfying himself with resolutions of well-doing, he had actually gone to work and made a good practical beginning.

Too many are, however, impatient of results. They are not satisfied to begin where their fathers did, but where they left off. They think to enjoy the fruitts of industry without working for them. They cannot wait for the results of labor and application, but forestall them by too early indulgence. A worthy Scotch couple, when asked how their son had broken down so early in life, gave the following explanation: "When we began life together, we worked hard, and lived upon porridge and such like, gradually adding to our comforts as our means improved, until we were able at length to dine off a bit of roast meat, and sometimes a boilt chuckie (or fowl); but as for Jock, our son, he began where we had left off—*he began wi' the chuckie first.*" The same illustration will apply to higher conditions of life than that of this humble pair.

Middle class people are too apt to live up to their incomes, if not beyond them; affecting a degree of "style" which is most unhealthy in its effect upon society at large. There is an ambition to bring up boys as gentlemen, or rather "genteel" men; though the result frequently is, only to make them gents. They acquire a taste for dress, style, luxuries, and amusements, which can never form any solid foundation for manly or gentlemanly character; and the result is, that we have a vast number of gingerbread young gentry thrown upon the world, who remind one of the abandoned hulls sometimes picked up at sea, with only a monkey on board.

There is a dreadful ambition abroad for being "genteel." We keep up appearances, too often at the expense of honesty; and, though we may not be rich, yet we must seem to be so. We must be "respectable," though only in the meanest sense—in mere vulgar outward show. We have not the courage to go patiently onward in the condition of life in which it has pleased God to call us; but must needs live in some fashionable state to which we ridiculously please to call ourselves, and all to gratify the vanity of that unsubstantial genteel world of which we form a part. There is a constant struggle and pressure for front seats in the social amphitheatre; in the midst of which all noble self-denying resolve is trodden down, and many fine natures are inevitably crushed to death. What waste, what misery, what bankruptcy, come from all this ambition to dazzle others with the glare of apparent worldly success, we need not describe. The mischievous results show themselves in a thousand ways—in the rank frauds committed by men who dare to be dishonest, but do not dare to seem poor; and in the desperate dashes at fortune, in which the pity is not so much for those who fail, as for the hundreds of innocent families who are so often involved in their ruin.

To be above the necessity of labor,—to spend life in doing nothing,—is the fancied paradise of many youthful minds. Yielding to these illusive dreams, they cultivate a hatred for labor; they view the necessity which binds them to the counting-room or the workshop as the galley-slave regards his chain. They envy every gay son of pleasure whose empty laugh is heard ringing through the street. Hence their labor is irksome—their temper sour and repulsive. Their manners become insulting and vexatious to their employers; their incessant complainings annoy their parents, and misery spreads throughout the entire circle of their influence. Thousands of parental hearts are aching at this moment, and thousands of employers are unhappy with their apprentices, solely from this foolish, guilty aspiration after *nothing to do* which haunts the imaginations of so many young men.

Great men have ever been men of thought, as well as men of action. As the magnificent river, rolling in the pride of its mighty waters, owes its greatness to the hidden springs of the mountain nook, so does the wide-sweeping influence of distinguished men date its origin from hours of privacy, resolutely employed in efforts after self-development. The invisible spring of self-culture is the source of every great achievement.

Away, then, young man, with all dreams of superiority unless you are determined to dig after knowledge, as men search for concealed gold! If you lack the resolution, the manly strength of purpose, needed to bind you to reading, reflection, and study, you may bid adieu to all hope of marked success. Your destiny is settled. You will dwell in ignoble nothingness, far down the vale of obscurity.

"An old man stood, on the night of a new

year, at his window, and gazed with the look of despair to the immovable, ever glowing heavens, and down to the calm, white earth, upon which there was no one so friendless and sleepless as he. For his grave lay near him; —it was covered only with the snow of old age, not with the green of youth, and he brought with him out of the rich abundance of his whole life nothing but errors, sins, and infirmities, a wasted body, a desolate soul, and an old age full of sorrow. To-day his beautiful youth days wandered about him like ghosts, and drew him back to that pleasant morning when his father first placed him on the cross-way of life which leads, on the right, by the sunny path of virtue in a broad peaceful land, full of light and harvests, and on the left, drags down in the mole track of vice into a black cavern full of dripping poison, hissing serpents, and dark, sultry vapors. As the serpents hung about his breast, and drops of poison upon his tongue, in unutterable grief and despair, he cried out to the heavens,— Give youth again! O Father, place me on that cross-way again, that I may choose another path. But his father and his youth were gone long ago. He saw wandering lights dancing among the marshes, and disappearing in the graveyard, and he said, These are my foolish and wasted days. He saw a star fall from heaven, and glimmer in its fall and vanish on the earth; I am that star, said the bleeding heart, and the serpent fangs of remorse struck deeper in his soul. His burning imagination pictured before him flying night-phantoms; and a skull, still lying in the tomb, by degrees assumed *his* look. In the midst of this struggle within him, the music for the new year flowed suddenly down from the church tower, like a far-off chant. His heart softened. He cast his eyes around the horizon and over the broad earth, and he thought of the friends of his youth, who now, happier than he, were bright examples of virtue and worth, fathers of happy children, and loved and honored by all around them, and he said, Oh, I might also like you have slept through this night with unwept eyes, if I had been willing. Ah, I might be happy, my dear parents, if I had followed your precepts. In this feverish remembrance of his youthful time, it seemed to him as if the skull, with the features of the tomb, raised itself up and became a living youth. He covered his eyes. A thousand scalding tears streamed down and disappeared in the snow. Hopeless in despair he yet only sighed in a low voice, —Come back again, O youth, come back. And it came back; for he had only dreamed so fearfully. He was still a young man. His grief alone had been no dream. But he thanked God that, still young, he could turn in the midst of the dark currents of life and reach the land of harvests. Turn back with him, young man, if you stand in his wandering way. This frightful dream will become in future your judge. But if ever full of sorrow and despair, you should cry out, Come again, bright and vigorous youth ; O come! Then it will not come again. It will be gone never to return."

VIII.

YOUNG WOMEN.

THE most important era in the life of a young woman is when she finally leaves school. At this time she begins to think for herself, and is left in more than ordinary freedom to act for herself. Up to this period, she has lived in obedience to parents, guardians, or teachers. She has gone to school, and pursued her studies under the entire direction of others, submitting her will and her judgment to the will and judgment of others, as older and wiser than herself. Her mind has been fully occupied with the various branches of knowledge which it has been deemed by others right that she should acquire. But now, books of instruction are laid aside; the strict rules of the seminary are no longer observed; the mind that has been for a long time active in the pursuits of knowledge sinks into repose.

Her whole future life will be affected by whatever is right or wrong in her conduct, and mode of thinking and living, at this period. The habits of order and study which existed while at school were not properly her own, for they were merely the result of obedience to laws prescribed by others; but now, acting in freedom, whatever she does is from herself, and stamps itself permanently upon the impressible substance of her forming character. If, from natural indolence, she sinks into idleness and self-indulgence, she will be in danger of forming a habit that will go with her through life; but if, from a sense of duty to herself and others, she still occupies all her time, and all the powers of her mind, in doing or acquiring something, she will gradually gain strength and force of character, as her mind expands, and take, as a woman, in a few years, a woman's true position of active use in her appropriate sphere.

Life is a voyage, and to most of us a rough and stormy one. In commencing this voyage, let each one emulate the wisdom, prudence, and forethought of the sailor. The weaker we are, and the less able to endure the shock of a tempest, the more careful should we be that everything is right before we push off from the shore.

It is clear, then, that, in the beginning of life a woman who has less ability to contend in the world, and is more exposed to evils and hardships, should reverses come, ought to furnish herself thoroughly with the means of self-sustenance and self-protection. This she can only do by acquiring some knowledge or skill, the exercise of which will enable her to supply not only her own wants, but the wants of all who may be dependent upon her. There is no time in which this can be done so well as in the few years which succeed the period of a young lady's final withdrawal from school. These years ought to be employed by all, no matter how high their station, in thoroughly mastering some branch of knowledge, or in acquiring some skill, from the exercise of which, as a regular employment, should necessity ever require it to be done, a livelihood may be obtained.

Viewing yourself in your relations to human society, you cannot fail to perceive much of evil, of danger, and of suffering, before you. You everywhere behold women whose early career was as gay, as secure, as promising, as your own, the victims of heart desolation, of acute suffering, of neglect, of poverty,—to whom life is as a desert waste, where suffocating winds sweep rudely past them, and stifling sands threaten to bury them in death. In one direction, you see a daughter thrown upon her own resources by the premature death of her parents; in another, a wife, but yesterday a happy bride, left to indescribable sorrow by the neglect of an unfaithful husband, or plunged into a mournful widowhood by the visitation of death.

Seek, therefore, young lady, for skill in household labors; acquire some means of living by your own labor; cultivate a courageous spirit; learn to be decided in your adhesion to the voices of duty,—and you will be fitted to confront, with a consciousness of strength to overcome them, the most trying ordeals of life. Resting on these qualities, you will feel strong, your heart will be bold, you will not sink, with a crushed and broken spirit, under the pressure of difficulty,—but, erect and mighty, you will be mistress of your circumstances, and victor over your trials.

While, if you despise the wisdom which distils from this advice,—if you live in slothful, idle self-neglect during the sunny hours of youth, and trouble suddenly bursts on your defenceless head,—

> "Your mind shall sink, a blighted flower,
> Dead to the sunbeam and the shower;
> A broken gem, whose inborne light
> Is scattered, ne'er to reunite."

Loveliness of spirit is woman's sceptre and sword, for it is both the emblem and the instrument of her conquests. Her influence flows from her sensibilities, her gentleness, her tenderness. It is this which disarms prejudice, and awakens confidence and affection in all who come within her sphere; which makes her more powerful to accomplish what her will resolves than if nature had endowed her with the strength of a giant.

I would not, however, have you to imagine, that loveliness of spirit alone is a source of high and abiding influence, nor that other great qualities may be dispensed with, if this one is obtained. So far is this from the truth, that this quality is dependent upon the existence of the most exalted moral excellencies. Nature may have endowed you with exquisite sensibility, with a highly refined and delicate physical organization, which may give you the appearance of being lovely, and enable you to make a favorable impression and to exert an irresistible power over the mind you aim to fascinate. But if your heart is lacking in high-minded self-devotion, in self-control, in sincerity, in genuine meekness, your loveliness, like a coating of gold upon a counterfeit coin, will disappear before all who behold you in contact with the realities of life. Genuine loveliness is the effulgence of sublime virtue; it is a soft and mellow light, diffusing a delicious radiance over the entire character, and investing its possessor with a halo of indefinable beauty. It is the "fresh ripple from deep fountains" of inborne love. It is the gentle dew descending from the clear heaven of a pure and lofty mind—the mystic charm that "pleases all around, from the wish to please."

Let every one see that you care for them by showing them what Sterne so happily calls "the small sweet courtesies of life," in which there is no parade; whose voice is too still to tease, and which manifest themselves by tender and affectionate looks and little acts of attention—giving others the preference in every little enjoyment at the table, in the field, walking, sitting or standing. This is the spirit that gives your sex its sweetest charm. It constitutes the sum total of the witchcraft of woman. Let the world see that your first care is for yourself, and you will spread the solitude of the upas-tree around you, in the same way, by the emanation of a poison which kills all the juices of affection in its neighborhood. Such a girl may be admired for her understanding and accomplishments, but she will never be beloved.

Self-culture implies suitable efforts to strengthen and expand the intellect, by reading, by reflection, and by writing down your thoughts. Reading suitable books stores the mind with facts and principles; reflection converts those facts and principles into a real mental aliment, and thus quickens the soul into growth; while writing tends to precision of thought and beauty of expression. Every young lady should, therefore, read much, reflect more, and write as frequently and carefully as she has opportunity.

The principal object of reading, with many young women, is pleasure. They seek for excited sensibilities and a charmed imagination. Hence, novels and poetry form the staple of their reading. Grave history, graver science, and dull philosophy they eschew, while they actually abhor the sober pages of theology. The novel is well thumbed; the poem, if it is not too Miltonic, is well turned down at the corners; but poor Gibbon, Mosheim, Newton, lie quietly in some snug corner, robed in cobwebs, beside the dust-covered and despised Bible. What is the consequence? Obscured, feeble intellect, a weakened memory, an extravagant and fanciful imagination, benumbed sensibilities, a demoralized conscience and a corrupted heart! A troop of evils more to be dreaded by a young lady than the advance of an invading army—for soldiers only kill the body, but these strangle the immortal mind.

Learn to become the good, guardian genius of the opposite sex. Breathe hope, vigor, encouragement into all hearts that live around you. But, to do this, you must be brave yourself. You require a strong, trustful, courageous spirit in your own breast. You need to carefully cultivate it, by subduing fear and laboring to rise equal to your present emergencies. It is not fear alone, but fear unrestrained, that makes a coward; nor is bravery the absence of fear.

A young lady would shrink appalled at the idea of daily puncturing her brother's eye with a needle, to the destruction of his sight, yet will breathe a spirit of discontent, pride, and folly into his mind; and thus, by disturbing his happiness at home, drive him to seek congenial society abroad, where his morals grow depraved, his character is lost, and his soul ruined. This fearful result she brings about, without a sigh of regret or a pang of sorrow. When the evil work is done she weeps over the wreck, and would give the gold of the world to restore the fallen one. Yet for her share in causing this destruction she sheds not a tear; indeed, she is unconscious that any portion of the blame lies at her door. Her influence was silent and invisible when in exercise, and yet it drove her brother to ruin.

Your image will stand before a brother, a

husband or a father, as a good genius in the hour of temptation, and forbid the triumph of the tempter. For, calling up your character, his full heart will exclaim of you:—

> "She looks as whole as some serene
> Creation minted in the golden moods
> Of sovereign artists; not a thought, a touch,
> But pure as lines of green that streak the white
> Of the first snow-drop's inner leaves."

In order that a young lady may be qualified to act well her part in life, she should acquire a thorough knowledge of all domestic and culinary affairs, so that, even if she should never be required by circumstances to go into the kitchen to cook a dinner, she will yet be able to give directions how to do it, and know when it is properly done. No one knows what a day may bring forth. Life is a scene of perpetual changes. We have known ladies who have been raised in entire freedom from labor, suddenly reduced to poverty, and compelled, for a time, to do what might well be called household drudgery, or see their husbands and children subjected to the severest privations. And even where no such reverse, but only a change from one section of the country to another, has taken place, the necessity for a practical knowledge of everything pertaining to housekeeping is frequently found to exist.

No hand but the hand of a wife should prepare the food of her husband when he is sick; and no hand but the hand of a mother, the food of her child. A remembrance of the badly-prepared, tasteless food, which almost every woman has had served to her in sickness, from her own cook, will be felt as a sufficient reason for this declaration. To cook for the sick requires an experienced hand. A woman who knows nothing at all about cooking will fail entirely in the attempt, and if her husband be sick, he will be fortunate, indeed, if he can take more than a few spoonfuls of the tea, or a few morsels of the toast, that is brought to his bedside as he begins to convalesce.

If for no other purpose, a young lady should learn the art of cooking in order that she may be able to prepare the food of her parent, her brother, her sister, or, at some future time, the food of her husband, when sick. This may seem a little matter. But no one who has been sick will think it so. It must not be inferred that we would shut every woman up, a prisoner in her house, and cause her to devote every hour of her time to domestic duties. All we contend for is, that a woman should govern in her household, as fully as a man governs in his store, office, counting-room, manufactory, or workshop, and that in order to do this, she should qualify herself beforehand for her particular duties, as he has to qualify himself for his.

A young man, remarkable for his strong good sense, married a very accomplished and fashionable young lady, attracted more by her beauty and accomplishments than by anything else. In this, it must be owned that his strong good sense did not seem very apparent. His wife, however, proved to be a very excellent companion, and was deeply attached to him, though she still loved company, and spent more time abroad than he exactly approved. But, as his income was good, and his house furnished with a full supply of domestics, he was not aware of any abridgments of comfort on this account, and he therefore made no objection to it.

One day, some few months after his marriage, our friend, on coming home to dinner, saw no appearance of his usual meal, but found his wife in great trouble instead.

"What's the matter?" he asked.

"Maggie went off at ten o'clock this morning," replied his wife, "and the chambermaid knows no more about cooking a dinner than the man in the moon."

"Couldn't she have done it under your direction?" inquired the husband, very coolly.

"Under *my* direction? Goodness! I should like to see a dinner cooked under my direction."

"Why so?" asked the husband in surprise. "You certainly do not mean that you cannot cook a dinner."

"I certainly do, then," replied his wife. "How should I know anything about cooking?"

The husband was silent, but his look of astonishment perplexed and worried his wife.

"You look very much surprised," she said after a moment or two had elapsed.

"And so I am," he answered, "as much surprised as I should be at finding the captain on one of my ships unacquainted with navigation. Don't know how to cook, and the mistress of a family! Belle, if there is a cooking school any where in the city, go to it, and complete your education, for it is deficient in a very important particular."

The wife was hurt and offended at the words and manner of her husband; but she soon got over this. The next time the cook went away there was no trouble about the dinner.

Order, is the essential prerequisite of every truly efficient action. Without it, nothing can be done well; with it, there is no duty in life that may not be rightly performed. Without it, the lightest task is burdensome; with it, that which to look at seems almost herculean becomes a matter of easy accomplishment.

Neatness almost invariably accompanies order; indeed, the one is nearly inseparable from the other. When we see a neat person, we expect to find one who is orderly in all her habits, and we are rarely mistaken. Neatness in dress should be regarded as much as neatness in every thing that is done. A want of neatness, as well as a want of order, shows a

defect in the mind, the correction of which is essential to happiness. The only way to correct any such defect is to *act* in opposition to it.

But let it not be forgotten that the habit of order must be formed in early years. When life's most serious duties press upon the mind, and demand the exercise of all its energies, there is no time to think about systems of order, and little inclination to attempt doing so.

IX.

BROTHERS AND SISTERS.

YOUNG man, if you have sisters, who are just entering society, all your interest should be awakened for them. You cannot but have made the discovery, that too few of the young men who move about in the various social circles are fit associates for a pure-minded woman. Their exterior, it is true, is very fair; their persons are elegant, and their manners attractive; but you have met them when they felt none of the restraints of female society, and seen them unmask their real characters. You have heard them speak of this sweet girl, and that pure-minded woman, in terms that would have roused your deepest indignation, had your own sister been the subject of allusion.

You may know all these things, but your

innocent sisters at home cannot know them, nor see reason for shunning the society of those whose real characters, if revealed, would cause them to turn away in disgust and horror. From the dangers of an acquaintanceship with such young men, it is your duty to guard your sisters; and you must do this more by warding off the evil than by warnings against it. In order to do this, you should make it a point of duty always to go with your sisters into company, and to be their companion, if possible, on all public occasions. By so doing, you can prevent the introduction of men whose principles are bad; or, if such introductions are forced upon them in spite of you, can throw in a timely word of caution. This latter it may be too late to do after an acquaintanceship is formed with a man whose character is detestable in your eyes. Your sister will hardly believe that one who is attractive in all respects, and who can converse of virtue and honor so eloquently, can possibly have an impure or vicious mind. The great thing is to guard, by every means in your power, these innocent ones from the polluting presence of a bad man. You cannot tell how soon he may win the affections of the most innocent, confiding, and loving of them all, and draw her off from virtue. And even if his designs be honorable, if he win her but to wed her, her lot will be by no means an enviable one; for no pure-minded woman ever has been, or ever can be made happy by a corrupt, evil-minded, and selfish man. On your faithfulness to your duty may depend a lifetime of happiness or misery for those who are, or ought to be, very dear to you. Your affection for them should lead you to enter into their pleasures as far as in your power to do so; to give interest and variety to the home circle; to afford them, at all times, the assistance of your judgment in matters of trivial as well as grave importance. By this, you will gain their confidence and acquire an influence over them that may, at some later period, enable you to serve them in a moment of impending danger.

We very often see young men with sisters, who appear to be entirely indifferent in regard to them. They rarely visit together; their associates are strangers to each other; they appear to have no common interests. This state of things is the fault, nine times in ten, of the young men. It is the result of their neglect and indifference. There are very few sisters who do not with a most tender and unselfish regard love their brothers, especially their elder brothers, and who would not feel happier in being their companions than in the companionship of almost any one else. Notwithstanding all this neglect and indifference, how willingly is every little office performed that adds to the brother's comfort! How much care is there for him, who gives back so little in return!

A regard for himself, as well as for his sisters, should lead a young man to be much with them. Their influence in softening, polishing, and refining his character will be very great. They have perceptions of the propriety and fitness of things far quicker than he has; and this he will soon see if he observe their remarks upon the persons with whom they come in contact, and the circumstances that transpire around them. While he is reasoning on the subject, and balancing many things in his mind before coming to a satisfactory conclusion, they, by a kind of intuition, have settled the whole matter, and settled it, he will find, truly.

The temptations to which young men are exposed, when first they come in contact with the world, are many, and full of the strongest allurements. Their virtuous principles are assailed in a thousand ways; sometimes boldly, and sometimes by the most insidious arts of the vicious and evil-minded. All, therefore, that can make virtue lovely in their eyes, and vice hideous, they need to strengthen the good principles stored up, from childhood, in their minds. For their sakes, home should be made as attractive as possible, in order to induce them frequently to spend their evenings in the place where, of all others, they will be safest. To do this, a young lady must consult the tastes of her brothers, and endeavor to take sufficient interest in the pursuits that interest them, so as to make herself companionable.

There is no surer way for a sister to gain an influence with her brother, than to cultivate all exterior graces and accomplishments, and improve her mind by reading, thinking, and observation. By these means she not only becomes his intelligent companion, but inspires him with a feeling of generous pride towards her, that, more than anything else, impresses her image upon his mind, brings her at all times nearer to him, and gives her a double power over him for good.

The indifference felt by brothers towards their sisters, when it does exist, often arises from the fact that their sisters are inferior, in almost everything, to the women they are in the habit of meeting abroad. Where this is the case, such indifference is not so much to be wondered at.

Sisters should always endeavor to gain, as much as possible, the confidence of their brothers, and to give them their confidence in return. Mutual good offices will result from this, and attachments that could only produce unhappiness may be prevented. A man sees more of men than a woman does, and the same is true in regard to the other sex. This being so, a brother has it in his power at once to guard his sister against the advances of an unprincipled man, or a man whose habits he knows to be bad, and a sister has it in her power to reveal to her brother traits of character in a woman, for whom he is about forming an attachment, that would repel rather than attract him.

If your brothers are younger than you, encourage them to be perfectly confidential with you; win their friendship by your sympathy in all their concerns, and let them see that their interests and their pleasures are liberally provided for in the family arrangements. Never disclose their little secrets, however unimportant they may seem to you; never pain them by an ill-timed joke; never repress their feelings by ridicule, but be their tenderest friend, and then you may become their ablest adviser. If separated from them by the course of school and college education, make a point of keeping up your intimacy by full, free, and affectionate correspondence; and when they return to the paternal roof, at that awkward age between youth and manhood, when reserve creeps over the mind like an impenetrable veil, suffer it not to interpose between you and your brothers. Cultivate their friendship and intimacy with all the address and tenderness you possess; for it is of unspeakable importance to them that their sisters should be their confidential friends. Consider the loss of a ball or party, for the sake of making the evening pass pleasantly to your brothers at home, as a small sacrifice—one you should unhesitatingly make. If they go into company with you, see that they are introduced to the most desirable acquaintances, and show them that you are interested in their acquitting themselves well.

So many temptations beset young men, of which young women know nothing, that it is of the utmost importance that your brothers' evenings should be happily passed at home; that their friends should be your friends; that their engagements should be the same as yours; and that various innocent amusements should be provided for them in the family circle. I know no more agreeable and interesting spectacle than that of brothers and sisters playing and singing together those elevated compositions in music and poetry which gratify the taste and purify the heart, while their parents sit delighted by. I have seen and heard an elder sister thus leading the family choir, who was the soul of harmony to the whole household, and whose life was a perfect example of those virtues which I am here endeavoring to inculcate. Let no one say, in reading this chapter, that too much is here required of sisters; that no one can be expected to lead such a self-sacrificing life.

I have been told by men, who had passed unharmed through the temptations of youth, that they owed their escape from many dangers to the intimate companionship of affectionate and pure-minded sisters. They have been saved from a hazardous meeting with idle company by some home engagement, of which their sisters were the charm; they have refrained from mixing with the impure, because they would not bring home thoughts and feelings which they could not share with those trusting and loving friends; they have put aside the wine-cup, and abstained from stronger potations, because they would not profane with their fumes the holy kiss, with which they were accustomed to bid their sisters good-night.

X.

MAN.

TO be great is to be good, to be good is to be wise, and to be wise is to know thyself. "Know thyself" is a precept which, we are informed, descended from Heaven. It is a noble science to know one's self; and a noble courage to know how to yield.

The Arabs have a proverb, "The moment a man is satisfied with himself, everybody else is dissatisfied with him." We have weak points both by birth and education, and it may be questioned which of the two give us the most trouble. If we were as careful to polish our manners as our teeth, to make our temper sweet as our breath, to cut off our faults as to pare our nails, to be upright in character as in person, to shave our souls as to shave our chin, what an immaculate race we should become! Many a man thinks it is a virtue that keeps him from turning rascal, when it is only a full stomach. One should be careful and not mistake potatoes for principles. If it is difficult to see any fault in a child, or a book, or a pudding, or any one we love, how much more so that we should see any in ourselves!

There is nothing that helps a man in his conduct through life more than a knowledge of his own characteristic weakness, which, guarded against, becomes his strength, as there is nothing that tends more to the success of a man's talents than his knowing the limits of his faculties, which are thus concentrated on some practical object. One man can do but one thing well. Universal pretensions end in nothing. It is a deplorable condition, to be always doing what we are always condemning. The reproaches of others are painful enough. But when the lash is laid on by our own hand, the anguish is intolerable. How cheering, on the contrary, even in the deepest night of calamity, when conscience calls out from her watch-tower in the soul—*All's Well!*

Just and discriminating ideas generally lead to proper action, and a willing judgment enforces a strict adherence to the rules of propriety. Stupid, yes *presumptuous* must that man be who would peril every consideration for a good character upon a base act, simply because he cannot see at once the true tendency of a consistent course of life. But it *can* be seen, and like the works of a good man, will shine before the world, leaving a light behind, and sending its arrowy beams into the future, to guide life's wandering steps aright.

Deportment, honesty, caution, and a desire to do right carried out in practice, are to human character what truth, reverence, and love are to religion. They are the unvaried elements of a good reputation. Such virtues can never be reproached, although the vulgar and despicable may scoff at them; but it is not so much in their affected revulsion at them, as it is in the wish to reduce them to the standard of their own degraded natures, and vitiated passions. Let such scoff and sneer,—let them laugh and ridicule as much as they may,—a strict, upright, onward course will evince to the world and to them, that there is more manly independence in one forgiving smile, than in all the pretended exceptions to worthiness in the society of the mean and vulgar. Virtue must have its admirers, and firmness of principle, both moral and religious, will ever command the proudest encomium of the intelligent world, to the exclusion of every other thing connected with human existence.

There is no surer destroyer of youth, privileges, powers and delights,— than yielding the spirit to the empire of ill-temper and selfishness. We should all be cautious, as we advance in life, of allowing occasional sorrowful experience to overshadow our preception of the preponderance of good. Faith in good is at once its own rectitude and reward. To believe good, and to do good, truly and trustfully, is the healthiest of humanity's conditions. To take events cheerfully, and promote the happiness of others is the way to ensure the enduring spring of existence. Content and kindliness are the soft vernal showers and fostering sunny warmth that keep a man's nature and being fresh and green.

Sociality is to man what modesty is to woman; it is a principle that should be ever active, but governed by occasion and consistency. A lack of this betrays at once a deficiency in true manliness. Not so much depends upon a power or faculty as upon its proper exercise, and when this is abused, there is a great depreciation of its beauties. To the young man just entering the most important portion of his existence—the formation of a worthy name and character—it is well that he should first learn that society corrupts as it is corrupt—that it forms or moulds principles by a gradual or accelerated progress according to the degree of its influence.

Man is to be rated, not by his hoards of gold, not by the simple or temporary influence he may for a time exert; but by his unexceptionable principles relative both to character and religion. Strike out these, and what is he? A brute without a virtue—a savage without a sympathy! Take them away and his *manship* is gone; he no longer lives in the image of his Maker! A cloud of sin hangs darkly on his brow; there is ever a tempest on his countenance, the lightning in his glance, the thunder in words, and the rain and whirlwind in the breathing of his angry soul. No smile gladdens his lip to tell that love is playing there; no sympathizing glow illuminates his cheek. Every word burns with malice, and that voice—the mystic gift of Heaven—grates as harshly on the timid ear, as rushing thunders beating amid falling cliffs and tumbling cataracts.

But this is too dark a picture for a long continued view. Turn we from it now, as from a frightful scene, to the only divine image that Virtue elevates before the world for example and imitation. Let man go abroad with just principles, and what is he? An exhaustless fountain in a vast desert! A glorious sun shining ever—dispelling every vestige of darkness! There is love animating his heart, sympathy breathing in every tone. Tears of pity—dew drops of the soul—gather in his eye, and gush impetuously down his cheek. Quivering on his lips are words that wait for utterance, and thoughts, winged as with lightning, play amid his tell-tale glances. A good man is abroad and the world knows and feels it. Beneath his smile lurks no degrading passion; within his heart there slumbers no guile. He is not exalted in mortal pride—not elevated in his own views, but honest, moral and virtuous before the world. He stands throned on truth, his fortress is wisdom and his dominion is the vast and limitless universe. Always upright, kind and sympathizing, always attached to just principles and actuated by the same, governed by the highest motives in doing good—*these are his only* TRUE MANLINESS.

XI.

WOMAN.

WOMAN is a very nice and a very complicated machine. Her springs are infinitely delicate, and differ from those of a man as the work of a repeating watch does from that of a town clock. Look at her body—how delicately formed! Observe her understanding, how subtle and acute! But look into her heart—there is the watchwork, composed of parts so minute in themselves, and so wonderfully combined, that they must be seen by a microscopic eye to be clearly comprehended. The perception of woman is as quick as lightning. Her penetration is intuition—I had almost said instinct. A woman's whole life is a history of the affections. The heart is her world; it is there her ambition strives for empire; it is there her avarice seeks for hidden treasures. She sends forth her sympathies on adventure; she embarks her whole soul in the traffic of affection; and if shipwrecked, her case is hopeless—for it is bankruptcy of the heart.

To feel, to love, to suffer, to devote herself, will always be the text of the life of woman.

Woman's influence is the sheet anchor of society; and this influence is due, not exclusively to the fascination of her charms, but chiefly to the strength, uniformity and consistency of her virtues, maintained under so many sacrifices, and with so much fortitude and heroism. Without these endowments and qualifications, external attractions are nothing; but with them, their power is irresistible. Beauty and virtue are the crowning attributes bestowed by nature upon woman, and the bounty of heaven more than compensates for the injustice of man. The possession of these advantages secures to her universally that degree of homage and consideration which renders her independent of the effects of unequal and arbitrary laws. But it is not the incense of idle worship which is most acceptable to the heart of woman; it is, on the contrary, the just appreciation of her proper position, merits, and character. What man expects to acquire by force of energy and the exercise of his talents, woman hopes to obtain by the power of pleasing, and her ascendency over the heart. The means are different, the ends in view the same; namely, prosperity in life, and a desirable position in the world. There is no period in the life of man, as long as his mental and bodily powers remain unimpaired, in which he is socially disqualified for the race he has to run, and that contest in which he is called upon to engage. He may remain a long time a silent, but watchful spectator of the scene; or he may be disabled, and thrown off his balance; but he can appear again, and by summoning his dormant faculties to his aid, he may succeed in dividing the booty with his compeers, or in securing his share of the world's honor and spoils. To place a woman in early life in a career like this, is to alter her destiny, to endanger her respectability, to destroy her sympathies, and to subvert the intentions of Nature. If, by the influence of her charms, or the opportunities of her position, she has failed to procure a desirable elevation in society—or if, by a cruel destiny, she has been deprived of friends and fortune, and is urged to assert her rights, and to make her own way through the world—if her resolution can save her from despair, and her principles of virtue from reproach—yet she labors under great disadvantages in placing herself upon the same footing with men, who are hardened to the world, and more accustomed to personal privations and toil. But nevertheless, there have been women who, impelled by high motives and a determined sense of duty, have surmounted all these obstacles, and have acquired by their own efforts both fortune and influence. Some moralist has said that no woman had a right to be plain; which is true. Her nature entitles her to be beautiful only, and when it is really operative always renders her so. Never yet saw any one beauty in woman which was not purely womanly, and therefore, impersonal. The person who reveals it, joyously feels herself to be merely the priestess or minister of this sacred flame, and shrinks from all personal property in it, as from sacrilege.

The men who flatter women do not know

them sufficiently; and the men who only abuse them do not know them at all. America is the Paradise of women. They are more respected, honored and loved, and more tenderly treated, in this country than in any other on earth. In other lands, women, in many instances, and in some constantly, toil in the fields like beasts of burden, while their fathers, and husbands, and brothers, and sons sit smoking and drinking at home, or in the public bar-room, thus squandering in dissipation the pittance so hardly earned by the females of the family. What makes those men who associate habitually with women, superior to others? What makes that woman who is accustomed and at ease in the society of men, superior to her sex in general? Solely because they are in the habit of free, graceful, continued conversation with the other sex. Women in this way lose their frivolity; their faculties awaken; their delicacies and peculiarities unfold all their beauty and captivation in the spirit of intellectual rivalry.

The mind of woman is peculiarly constituted, and exquisitely adapted for playing upon and influencing the finer parts of man's nature;

and whenever the heart of man is dead to influence, it is dead to almost every higher and purer feeling which alone distinguishes him from the beasts of the forest. As women are respected by the men of the age, so may, from time to time, be traced by an unerring measure, the degree of civilization to which that generation has attained.

Emerson says, "We consider man the representative of intellect, and the woman as the representative of affection; but each shares the characteristic of the other, only in the man one predominates, and in the woman the other. We know woman as affectionate, as religious, as oracular, as delighting in grace and order, possessed of taste. In all ages, woman has been the representative of religion. In all countries it is the women who fill the temples. In every religious movement the woman has had an active and powerful part, not only in the most civilized, but in the most uncivilized countries; not less in the Mohammedan than the Greek and Roman religions. She holds man to religion. There is no man so reprobate, so careless of religious duty, but that he delights to have his wife a saint.

All men feel the advantages that abound of that quality in a woman. My own feeling is that in all ages woman has held substantially the same influence. I think that superior women are rare. I think that women feel when they are in the press, as men of genius are said to do among energetic workers—that they see through all these efforts with finer eyes than their noisy masters. I think that all men in the presence of the best women feel overlooked and judged, and sometimes sentenced. They are the educators in all our society. Through their sympathy and quickness they are the proper mediators between those who have knowledge and those who want it."

Whatever may be the customs and laws of a country, the women of it decide the morals. They reign because they hold possession of our affections. But their influence is more or less salutary, according to the degree of esteem which is granted them. Whether they are our idols or companions, the reaction is complete, and they make us such as they are themselves. It seems as if nature connected our intelligence with their dignity, as we connect our morality with their virtue. This, therefore, is a law of eternal justice: Man cannot degrade a woman without himself falling into degradation; he cannot raise them without himself becoming better. Let us cast our eyes over the globe, and observe those two great divisions of the human race, the east and the west. One-half of the ancient world remain without progress or thought, and under the load of a barbarous cultivation; women there are serfs. The other half advance towards freedom and light; the women are loved and honored.

The influence which woman exerts is silent and still, felt rather than seen, not chaining the hands, but restraining our actions by gliding into the heart.

He cannot be an unhappy man who has the love and smile of woman to accompany him in every department of life. The world may look dark and cheerless without — enemies may gather in his path—but when he returns to his fireside, and feels the tender love of woman, he forgets his cares and troubles, and is a comparatively happy man. He is but half prepared for the journey of life, who takes not with him that friend who will forsake him in no emergency—who will divide his sorrows—increase his joys — lift the veil from his heart—and throw sunshine amid the darkest scenes. No man can be miserable who has such a companion, be he ever so poor, despised, and trodden upon by the world.

Mysterious woman! Place her among flowers, foster her as a tender plant, and she is a thing of fancy, waywardness, and sometimes folly—annoyed by a dew drop, fretted by the touch of a butterfly's wing, and ready to faint at the rustle of a beetle; the zephyrs are too rough, the showers too heavy, and she is overpowered by the perfume of a rose-bud. But let real calamity come—rouse her affection — enkindle the fires of her heart, and mark her then; how her heart strengthens itself—how strong is her purpose. Place her in the heat of battle—give her a child, a bird—anything she loves or pities, to protect—and see her, as in a relative instance, raising her white arms as a shield, as her own blood crimsons her upturned forehead, praying for life to protect the helpless. Transplant her in the dark places of earth—awaken her energies to action, and her breath becomes a healing—her presence a blessing. She disputes, inch by inch, the strides of the stalking pestilence, when man, the strong and brave, shrinks away, pale and affrightened. Misfortune daunts her not; she wears away a life of silent endurance, and goes forward with less timidity than to her bridal. In prosperity she is a bud full of odors, waiting but for the winds of adversity to scatter them abroad—pure gold, valuable, but united in the furnace. In short—woman is a miracle—a mystery, the center from which radiates the great charm of existence. Under the most depressing circumstances woman's weakness becomes fearless courage, all her shrinking and sinking passes away, and her spirit acquires the firmness of marble — adamantine firmness, when circumstances drive her to put forth all her energies under the inspiration of her affections.

Nothing can be more touching than to behold a woman who had been all tenderness and dependence, and alive to every trivial roughness while treading the prosperous paths of life, suddenly rising in mental force to be the comforter and supporter of her husband under misfortune, and abiding with unshrinking firmness the bitterest winds of adversity. As the vine which has long twined its graceful foliage about the oak, and been lifted by it in sunshine, will, when the hardy plant is rived by the thunderbolt, cling round it with its caressing tendrils, and bind up its scattered boughs; so it is beautifully ordained that woman, who is the mere dependent and ornament of man in happiest hours, should be his stay and solace when smitten by sudden calamity.

XII.

HOME.

A SINGLE bitter word may disquiet an entire family for a whole day. One surly glance casts a gloom over the household, while a smile, like a gleam of sunshine, may light up the darkest and weariest hours. Like unexpected flowers, which spring up along our path, full of freshness, fragrance and beauty, do kind words and gentle acts and sweet dispositions, make glad the home where peace and blessing dwell. No matter how humble the abode, if it be thus garnished with grace and sweetened with kindness and smiles, the heart will turn lovingly toward it from all the tumult of the world, will be the dearest spot beneath the circuit of the sun.

And the influences of home perpetuate themselves. The gentle grace of the mother lives in the daughter long after her head is pillowed in the dust of death; and the fatherly kindness feels its echo in the nobility and courtesy of sons, who come to wear his mantle and to fill his place; while on the other hand, from an unhappy, misgoverned and disordered home, go forth persons who shall make other homes miserable, and perpetuate the sourness and sadness, the contentions and strifes and railings which have made their own early lives so wretched and distorted.

Toward the cheerful home, the children gather "as clouds and as doves to their windows," while from the home which is the abode of discontent and strife and trouble, they fly forth as vultures to rend their prey.

The class of men who disturb and distress the world, are not those born and nurtured amid the hallowed influences of Christian homes; but rather those whose early life has been a scene of trouble and vexation,—who have started wrong in the pilgrimage, and whose course is one of disaster to themselves, and trouble to those around them.

Webster defines home as a "dwelling-place," but it admits of a broader meaning. There are brilliant and elegant homes. Some are wise, thrifty and careful, and others are warm and genial, by whose glowing hearths any one, at any time, may find enough and to spare. There are bright homes and gloomy homes. There are homes that hurry and bustle through years of incessant labor, until one and another of the inmates fall, like the falling leaves, and the homes turn to dust. We do not say the dairymaid's home compares with this last view. Science has done much to remove the drudgery in our homes, introducing ease and comfort. An ideal home must first have a government, but love must be the dictator. All the members should unite to make home happy. We should have light in our homes, heaven's own pure, transparent light. It matters not whether home is clothed in blue and purple, if it is only brimful of love, smiles, and gladness.

Our boards should be spread with everything good and enjoyable. We should have birds, flowers, pets, everything suggestive of sociability. Flowers are as indispensable to the perfections of a home as to the perfections of a plant. Do not give them all the sunniest windows and pleasantest corners, crowding out the children.

Of the ornamentation about a house, although a broad lake lends a charm to the scenery, it cannot compare with the babbling brook. As the little streamlet goes tumbling over the rocks and along the shallow, pebbly bed, it may be a marvelous teacher to the children, giving them lessons of enterprise and perseverance.

In our homes we must have industry and sympathy. In choosing amusements for the children, the latter element must be brought in. To fully understand the little ones, you must sympathize with them. When a child asks questions, don't meet it with, "Oh, don't bother me." Tell it all it wants to know. Never let your angry passion rise, no matter how much you may be tired. For full and intelligent happiness in the home circle, a library of the best works is necessary. Do not introduce the milk and water fiction of the present day, but books of character. Our homes should have their Sabbaths and their family altars. Around these observances cling many of the softest and most sacred memories of our lives.

A close observer of American life said to

us the other day that a great change had come in the last ten years to the home life of the country. And in answer to our interrogation, he proceeded to point out the character of this change. One point which he made was that a great many games of skill and chance were being played in New England homes, to-day, which were not known, or if known, were forbidden by parents ten years ago. Our own observation coincides with his on this point. We know that chess within the last ten years has captured for itself a high place in popular regard. It speaks well for a people when such an intellectual game can become popular. For it takes brains to play chess even moderately well, and none but clever and thoughtful people would ever like it. Checkers are not perhaps more universal, but they are more fashionable. They have fought their way into high life; and whereas they once found their friends in the village tavern and in the farmer's kitchen, they are now admitted into the parlors of the wealthy and refined. The games played with historical cards are also numerous and many of them pleasantly exciting. And you find them in almost every household. Now all this is very pleasant and hopeful. It reveals to the thinker the fact that home life is more vivacious and happy than it used to be; that the long dull evenings are being enlivened with sprightly and stimulating amusements, and that the home circle is charged with attractions which it once sadly lacked. These games are helping to make the homes of the country happier, helping to make the children more contented with their homes, and in doing this they are helping to make the country more intelligent and more virtuous. By wise parents these games are looked upon as God-sends. They help solve the problem of home amusements and recreation; and this, as all parents know, is one of the greatest problems they have to solve. Parents, make your homes as happy as you possibly can for your children and their mates. Fill them with fun and frolic and the cheerfulness of spirited social life. Play these games with your children yourselves, and thus share their joys with them; and feed your happiness on the spectacle of theirs. A great many homes are like the frame of a harp that stands without strings. In form and outline they suggest music; but no melody rises from the empty spaces; and thus it happens that home is unattractive, dreary and dull. Let us hope that this introduction of pleasant games—which will try both the wit and patience of the children, and of the older ones for that matter,—may become the fashion of the times, until every home in the land shall be perfectly furnished with these accessories of profit and pleasure. For the children's sake, let the reformation go on until every child shall have, in his father's house, be it humble or costly, such appliances and helps for his entertainment that he shall find his joy under his father's roof and in his father's presence.

"Home, home, sweet, sweet home,
Be it ever so humble, there is no place like home."

Among home amusements the best is the good old habit of conversation, the talking over the events of the day, in bright and quick play of wit and fancy, the story which brings the laugh, and the speaking the good and kind and true things, which all have in their hearts. It is not so much by dwelling upon what members of the family have in common, as bringing each to the ot er something interesting and amusing, that home life is to be made cheerful and joyous. Each one must do his part to make conversation genial and happy. We are too ready to converse with newspapers and books, to seek some companion at the store, hotel, or club-room, and to forget that home is anything more than a place to sleep and eat in. The revival of conversation, the entertainment of one another, as a roomful of people will entertain themselves, is one secret of a happy home. Wherever it is wanting, disease has struck into the root of the tree; there is a want which is felt with increasing force as time goes on. Conversation, in many cases, is just what prevents many people from relapsing into utter selfishness at their firesides. This conversation should not simply occupy husband and wife, and other older members of the family, but extend itself to the children. Parents should be careful to talk with them, to enter into their life, to share their trifles, to assist in their studies, to meet them in the thoughts and feelings of their childhood. It is a great step in education, when around the evening lamp are gathered the different members of a family, sharing their occupation with one another—the older assisting the younger, each one contributing to the entertainment of the other, and all feeling that the evening has passed only too rapidly away. This is the truest and best amusement. It is the healthy education of great and noble characters. There is the freedom, the breadth, the joyousness of natural life. The time spent thus by parents, in the higher entertainment of their children, bears a harvest of eternal blessings, and these long evenings furnish just the time.

It has been said, that a "man's manners form his fortune." Whether this be really so or not, it is certain that his manners form his reputation—stamp upon him, as it were, his current worth in the circles where he moves. If his manners are the products of a kind heart, they will please, though they be destitute of graceful polish. There is scarcely anything of more importance to a child of either sex, than good breeding. If parents and teachers perform their duties to the young faithfully, there will be comparatively few destitute of good manners.

Visit a family where the parents are civil and courteous toward all within their household, whether as dwellers or as guests, and their children will have good manners, just as they learn to talk, from imitation. But reverse the order of things concerning parents, and the children learn ill manners, just as in the former case they learn good manners, by imitation.

Train children to behave at home as you would have them act abroad. It is almost certain, that they, while children, conduct themselves abroad as they would have been in the habit of doing under like circumstances when at home. "Be courteous," is an apostolical injunction, which all should ever remember and obey.

There is sure to be contentment in a home, in the windows of which can be seen birds or flowers, and it may also be added that there will be the same conditions wherever there are pictures on the walls. It is, of course, not every one who is a judge of art, but even a contemplation of art will educate, and it is safe to say that a man cannot have a painting in his room and see it day after day without sooner or later beginning to be able to tell its merits or defects, and thus being better fitted to judge of others in the future. The engravings and chromos seen in the homes of the poor may, if measured by the critical rules of art, be wretched daubs, but they at least show a longing and an aspiration after beauty, while their presence helps to produce a repose of mind, and brings nothing with it but good. The loving manner in which children linger over pictures tells how deeply this feeling is implanted in the heart, and long before they can read, their dawning powers are gradually being strengthened by these silent educators.

Nor is the influence which flowers have, any less than that of paintings. At all seasons of the year they are gladly welcomed. They are emblematic of both the joys and sorrows of life, and religion has associated them with the highest spiritual verities. Faded although they sometimes may be, they have the power to wake the chords of memory and make us children again. At the sick bed and the marriage feast, on the altar and the cathedral walls, they have a meaning, and the humblest home looks brighter where they bloom. A few years ago, at horticultural societies in England, prizes were offered to villagers for the best efforts in cottage gardening, and the result was that a great change came over the home-life of the people. Instead of gardens filled with rank grass and weeds, there could be seen flaming hollyhocks, blood-red roses and purple geraniums, and a spirit of friendly rivalry and emulation was created, leading to improvements in households, and aiding habits of cleanliness and industry. Let any one walk through our markets on these bright spring mornings and watch how tenderly some poor seamstress will linger over a tiny flower and bear it away proudly to cheer the loneliness of her scantily furnished room, and he will admit that if such a little thing can bring pleasure or satisfaction, every effort made to improve the taste of the masses and lead them to make home pleasant is to be commended, as weakening the influence of evil and diffusing a power which will prove a potent factor for good.

Cherish the spirit of kindly affection. Let the love of childhood find a return, never repulsing the confiding tenderness every child displays when surrounded by kindly influences. Remember how much of the joy of life flows from the sympathetic mingling of congenial spirits, and seek to bind such to you closer and closer with the golden links of affection's easy bondage.

Cultivate singing in your family. Begin when the child is not yet three years old. The songs and hymns your childhood sang, bring them all back to your memory, and teach them to your little ones; mix them all together to meet the varying moods as in after life they come over us so mysteriously at times. Many a time, in the very whirl of business, in the sunshine and gayety of the avenue, amid the splendor of the drive in the park, some little thing wakes up the memories of early youth—the old mill, the cool spring, the shady tree by the little school-house—and the next instant we almost see again the ruddy cheeks, the smiling faces, and the merry eyes of schoolmates, some of whom are gray-headed now, while most have passed from amid earth's weary noises. And, anon, "the song my mother sang" springs unbidden to the lips, and soothes and sweetens all these memories. At other times, amid the crushing mishaps of business, a merry ditty of the olden time breaks in upon the ugly train of thought, and throws the mind in another channel; light breaks from behind the cloud in the sky, and new courage is given us. The honest man goes gladly to his work; and when, the day's labor done, his tools are laid aside and he is on his way home, where wife and child and the tidy table and cheery fireside await him, how can he but have music in his heart to break forth so often into the merry whistle or the jocund song? Moody silence, not the merry song, weighs down the dishonest tradesman, the perfidious clerk, the unfaithful servant, the perjured partner.

"We accord," says a gentleman who has written much, " our unqualified indorsement of the above; and even now, although we have passed our three-score years, the songs of our youth are often resurrected, and we love to hum them over again, and often do so, in the lone hours of the night when there are none to hear save ourself and the drowsy 'gray spiders on the wall;' and while doing so, we feel less inclined toward 'treason, stratagem, and spoils,' than at any other hour within the twenty-four. We fondly look back to the days when we were as musical as a hand organ—and perhaps as 'cracked' as many of them, too — those days when we so lightly touched the keys to the measure of the songs we sang. We often regret time, circumstance, and advancing years have so effectually quieted our vocal muse; still we revert to the ballads of yore, and mentally exclaim,

"'Sing me the songs that to me were so dear,
  Long, long ago ; long, long ago.'"

XIII.

FATHERS.

THERE is no time in a man's history when his relation is so sacred and peculiar to life as when the husband is merged into the father. The extent of this relation is so boundless and comprises so much, that he cannot fathom its depths or define its limits. The title is a heavenly inheritance. Our lips were early taught to lisp, "Our Father who art in Heaven." As the years rolled on we were more fully taught the nature and extent of this relationship. Perhaps the bitterest anguish a heart can know is to realize that it has done despite to that teaching and forgotten the Heavenly Father. Coupled with this reverential lesson was another, which is the duty and obligation we owed to our earthly father. The lips that gently whispered these lessons in drowsy ears, may now be silent and dumb. But did the impression then made fade or linger? The past will roll before us as a panorama: With what sensations shall we behold the several pictures slowly gliding by our mind's eye? What our life has been up to this time will answer this question. It must be a time

of solemnity and anxiety. Does the heart bound with lofty hopes and thrilling responsibilities; or is it saddened by depression and woe? It must in any event be a time of retrospection—a time to let into your hearts the perfect light of God's noonday. Does what you behold there sadden or satisfy you? This new page is added to your life—a new responsibility is opening before you. If your past has been what it should have been, you may look upon this new duty with awe indeed, but without terror. If, on the contrary, you look back upon a life of wasted opportunities, to constant rebellion to those naturally in authority over you, here is a grand time, and none "too late," to begin in a new. It is a God-given opportunity—another hostage to fortune. Your Heavenly Father will surely require it at your hands, and hold you to a strict accountability for its keeping.

A new and thrilling interest belongs to home, when family cares begin, when a new life takes up its abiding place within its sacred precincts. Husband and wife are not only what they were; new and sacred names belong to them. What an hour of deep, untold sensations, when parents look around thoughtfully upon offspring bearing their likeness, and having claims upon them as endearing as they are paramount.

The husband is the head of the wife, and,

in the home life, must be looked upon in a sense which clothes him with distinct and absolute stewardship. Many fathers claim the perquisites, but shirk the responsibilities of this relationship. What a tender, peculiar and chivalrous service he owes to the wife-mother! How royally should she be tended and guarded! What shall we say of a father who is remiss in his duty at this marked period of the home history! Whatever may have been his motive in choosing a wife, whether from caprice, cupidity, to better his social condition, or because the match was made in heaven; the whole after life of the father and mother will be colored, blessed or marred, by the relationship existing between them, prior and at the time when nature bestows the new titles. The husband, by his tender ministrations and manly devotions, may entrench himself within the innermost recesses of his companion's heart; and this, too, irrespective of any indifference of previous relationship. If there is ever a time when he can establish a firm hold upon her lifelong affection it is at this period in their history. And by his carelessness and insensibility, he may as easily win her everlasting and deserved contempt.

The father cannot be prophet, priest and king, as the revealed will of God makes him, without having centered in him all the responsibilities incidental to his prerogatives. His duty to the wife and mother, as important and far reaching as that duty is, must be considered also in relation to the whole family circle. This thought suggests another consideration, viz., his parental duty.

It is not necessary to enter upon any formal proof that there is such a thing. It is the dictate of reason. Revelation prescribes and guards it, with all the weight of its authority. The relationship between father and child is one of obligation as sacred and real as the moral duty which binds him to the God who made him. The fact of fatherly duty is then admitted. Nor is there much question of its extent within certain limits; for all are willing to do something for their children. "What man," says the Saviour, "is there of you whom, if his son ask for bread, will give him a stone?"

Children are human life, as property, entrusted into the hands of man. How shall we regard these repositories, and what account shall we render of our stewardship? Most men realize that they are not isolated from some relationship to the Heavenly Father, and that His all searching eye will discover every delinquency. There are some, however, who will look upon their vesture in this property from a different and more secular standpoint. Even such men owe it to themselves, to their own honor and the high qualities of humanity to train their children to be what they themselves wished they were. It is not necessarily the divine quality within man that urges him to provide for and take wise care of his offspring. The birds of the air are equally as careful in their way. They take the best bird care of their fledglings, and finally teach them to fly and do for themselves. It is absurd to reason with a man about an instinctive care that he would naturally take—so much is expected as a certainty. It is to the human and God-like quality that the appeal is made. He has no right to assume the fatherly responsibility unless he have a realizing sense of the obligation he is under to himself, to the child, to posterity, to time and eternity. When a man undertakes to measure and analyze such an accountability, he may become appalled, and yet the obligation need not be burdensome. Certain it is, he accepts the trust and he may so administer it that the occupation will be a perennial source of joy and gladness.

Every faculty, every passion, every capacity which the father possesses is at work in his children.

It is not only his peculiarities which they reflect, but his very nature. The image of the great model is mirrored in the nursery; and in its young thinkers, its embryo philosophers, its little architects and artists, its tiny heroes and heroines, its scenes of love and selfishness, is there outlined before his eyes, as a microscopic view, life in all its various phases. The child is coeval with the parent, and its destiny is as eternal as his own.

The father's power is not only extensive but peculiar as well.

There is no being for whom the child is disposed to feel more reverence than for his father. His father is to him the greatest of human beings. His father's authority, word or opinion, he is ready to put against the whole world. He never dreams of questioning the father's rights over him. It takes a long and sad time before the young spirit is darkened by the conviction that father is not very good, wise, and true. See how, when his great object of worship appears before him, reeling in intoxication, or uttering vile words, or yielding to some paroxysm of passion, the little judge will condemn very leniently. How ingenious he will be in finding excuses. His own early life and dawning prospects may be completely overshadowed, and, in a measure blighted, by some overwhelming disgrace on the father's part, and yet he is ever ready to fight that father's battles, with his puny arm but loving spirit. No one must question the father's character in his presence, and expect to escape punishment or rebuke. It takes years before he will admit that the father he has so tried to honor in his life and heart is either bad or foolish. What a pertinent commentary might be made here! If the child is so inherently loyal to the father, what should the father be to the child? What mighty possibilities are outlined by this fact! What clay ready for the hands of the father!

Nature's order ought not to be reversed. The child should not be father to the man.

Another peculiarity may be noticed. There is no one from whom the child will receive chastisement with such perfect absence of exasperation as from his father. Sent away from his presence in pain and in tears, it is one of nature's marvels that love still keeps its place; and soon the little offender will steal back again, yearning for the old kind look and affectionate embrace. Nay, a new tenderness will well up in the little soul toward you, humbly begging for forgiveness. They instinctively seem to forget their pain and disgrace, and to realize how painful it must have been to us, from the fullness of our great love, to inflict pain upon their bodies and hearts. They kiss the rod that smites. Let earthly fathers bear as humble and penitent a relation to the Father in Heaven; for he chasteneth every son he loveth. It evinces his love toward us, and sets the seal upon our relationship to him.

The father's power cannot be transferred nor delegated.

The father's power should be an absolute sovereignty. There is a species of so-called democratic freedom in this great country, that does not foster the best family discipline. In monarchical countries, the home government is somewhat patterned after the great civil model. It is less representative. There is but one head or fountain of power, and from that there is no appeal. It is well for the child to early learn to submit, without question, to some absolute and well-defined power, to become subservient to, and overshadowed by this power. The father loves them, and has a deep and tender interest in their welfare. He will exercise this wise control for their good. If children are not rendered fully amenable to this power, they may become a prey to the evil influence exerted over them by those who are not responsible for their well being, and have no interest in exercising this control wisely.

Fathers may not designedly delegate their power to others, yet by carelessness they suffer this power to lapse into the keeping of others.

Where is your child to-night? He may be in the world and not be of it. But that this may be so, he must be protected and guarded by home influences that will negative any evil influences from the outside. Think of tenderly nurtured youth parading the streets night after night, gazing in wonder upon the extreme attractions of gilded saloons or other haunts of vice! Think of the cynical remarks emanating from the lips of their associates! Think of the peculiar nature of the child that will not permit him to be one behind others of his associates in loud expressions and bold daring, and then estimate, if you can, how he is likely to be affected by this transferred power!

Fathers, keep your children at home. There may be mental and muttered rebellion against your dictum, but you know enough of life to realize that this is the best policy. What we have written may seem to apply more particularly to boys, but the girls are in just as much danger.

These girls are frequently attired in gaudy trappings and supposed to attend evening festive gatherings, where too much vanity is likely to be engendered. Keep the daughters at home. Their health and every consideration demands it. Keep the children at home till they are well grounded in the virtues and amenities of life, and then, when they do or must go from your presence and mingle in the world, they will be so surrounded by the subtle aroma of the gentler influences of the family circle that they will be impervious to anything base or low.

Finally, we would call attention to what many fathers regard as lost or unfulfilled opportunities.

The past may not be altogether retrieved, but it can give birth to a nobler future. You will look back to the time when you began this voyage of life. You had only to reach out to grasp every good thing in life. What father, that has arrived at mature years of accountability, has not had this dream of an ideal life! But, alas! how shortened we found our arms in the getting, and how many things that we thought were all and in all, become as dust in our grasp! These dreams were not entirely unfulfilled. It is well to aspire; for, though one may not obtain just what he sought, he secured more than he would if he aspired not at all. Some reach the goal, but those who have not, will sit down and reckon up the causes of failure. One may have been too heavily handicapped at the start; burdened with ill health or unpropitious surroundings. But he need not necessarily consider his life a failure—let such a father renew his youth in his children. He may remove from their path some of the obstacles that were insurmountable in his. The father owes this much to his children. The child must be an extraordinary one that ever arrives at goodness and greatness without some loving and fostering care. We often hear it said: "Oh, if I could only live my life over again!" Can the life not be lived again? Your children start with quite as many, if not more, advantages than did you. If you do your whole duty, exercising firmness and discretion, you can direct the attention of the children to the goal you yourself tried so ardently to reach. Let your mantle fall upon their shoulders. This is a worthy ambition.

XIV.

MOTHERS.

THE queen that sits upon the throne of home, crowned and sceptered as none other ever can be, is—mother. Her enthronement is complete, her reign unrivalled, and the moral issues of her empire are eternal. " Her children arise up, and call her blessed."

Rebellious, at times, as the subjects of her government may be, she rules them with marvellous patience, winning tenderness, and undying love. She so presents and exemplifies divine truth, that it reproduces itself in the happiest development of childhood — character and life.

Her memory is sacred while she lives, and becomes a perpetual inspiration, even when the bright flowers bloom above her sleeping dust. She is an incarnation of goodness to the child, and hence her immense power.

Scotland, with her well-known reverence for motherhood, insists that "An ounce of mother is worth more than a pound of clergy."

Napoleon cherished a high conception of a mother's power, and believed that the mothers of the land could shape the destinies of his beloved France. Hence he said in his sententious, laconic style: "The great need of France is mothers."

The ancient orator bestowed a flattering compliment upon the homes of Roman mothers when he said, "The empire is at the fireside." Who can think of the influence that a mother wields in the home, and not be impressed with its far-reaching results! What revolutions would take place in our families and communities if that strange, magnetic power were fully consecrated to the welfare of the child and the glory of God!

Mohammed expressed a great truth when he said that "Paradise is at the feet of mothers."

There is one vision that never fades from the soul, and that is the vision of mother and home. No man in all his weary wanderings ever goes out beyond the overshadowing arch of home.

Let him stand on the surf-beaten coast of the Atlantic, or roam over western wilds, and every dash of the wave and murmur of the breeze will whisper *home*, sweet home.

Set him down amid the glaciers of the North, and even there thoughts of home, too warm to be chilled by the eternal frosts, will float in upon him.

Let him rove through the green, waving groves, and over the sunny slopes of the South, and in the smile of the soft skies, and in the kiss of the balmy breeze, home will live again.

John Randolph was once heard to say that only one thing saved him from atheism, and that was the tender remembrance of the hour when a devout mother, kneeling by his side, took his little hand in hers, and taught him to say, " Our Father, who art in Heaven."

God hasten the time when our families, everywhere, shall catch the cry of childhood as it swells up over all the land, like the voice of God's own sweet evangel, calling the *home* —the home to enter the children's temple, and crowd its altars with the best offerings of sympathy and service.

The mother is the luminary that shines and

reigns alone in the early child-life; as years advance, the scepter is divided and the teacher shares the sway.

We often think, as we meet the earnest gaze of the interested pupil, and watch the mind working and the young thought shaping to the will, " Why is it that mothers so willingly yield to others this broad sphere of their domain, and are content to foster the physical and external life of their children, leaving the intellectual and spiritual to grow without their aid?"

One would suppose that capable mothers would jealously keep to themselves the high privilege of training the mind, and so bind their children to themselves by ties which are stronger than the mere physical tie can be.

We who have grown to realize to whom we are debtors, are thrilled with delight as we think of those who have been the parents of our intellectual life—who seem nearer to us than our familiar friends—Bryant, Longfellow, Ruskin, Emerson and Carlyle, and many another. How they have covered our lives with a rich broidery of beautiful and inspiring thought, so that to live in the same world, and at the same time, seems a blessing.

So may the mother weave into the life of her children thoughts and feelings, rich, beautiful, grand and noble, which will make all after-life brighter and better.

Many a good mother may think she has no time for this mind and soul culture, but we find no lack of robes and ruffles, and except in cases where the daily bread of the family must be earned by daily work, away from home, as is done by many a weary mother, we must feel that there is not one who cannot command one half hour each morning, when the mind is fresh and vigorous, to collect her children around her, and minister for a little to their higher wants.

Says that admirably pure writer, T. S. Arthur: "For myself, I am sure that a different mother would have made me a different man. When a boy I was too much like the self-willed, excitable C—; but the tenderness with which my mother always treated me, and the unimpassioned but earnest manner in which she reproved and corrected my faults, subdued my unruly temper. When I became restless or impatient, she always had a book to read to me, or a story to tell, or had some device to save me from myself. My father was neither harsh nor indulgent towards me; I cherish his memory with respect and love. But I have different feelings when I think of my mother. I often feel, even now, as if she were near me—as if her cheek were laid to mine. My father would *place his hand upon my head*, caressingly, but my mother would *lay her cheek against mine*. I did not expect my father to do more; for him it was a natural expression of affection. Her kiss upon my cheek, her warm embrace, are all felt now, and the older I grow, the more holy seem the influences that surrounded me in childhood."

All honor to mother! Without her smiles the world would lose its brightness—society's charm would exist no longer. Christianity would languish without her aid. "In whose principles," said the dying daughter of Ethan Allen to her sceptical father—" in whose principles shall I die — yours or my Christian mother's?" The stern old hero of Ticonderoga brushed away a tear from his eye as he turned away, and with the same rough voice which summoned the British to surrender, now tremulous with deep emotion, said —" in your

Christian mother's, child, in your mother's." Sacred to the heart is the memory of a mother's love.

Benjamin Franklin was accustomed to refer to his mother in the tenderest tone of filial affection. His respect and affection for her were manifested, among other ways, in frequent presents, that contributed to her comfort and solace in her advancing years. In one of his letters to her, for example, he sends her a *moidore*, a gold piece of the value of six dollars, "toward chaise hire," said he, "that you may ride warm to meetings during the winter." In another he gives her an account of the growth and improvement of his son and daughter—topics which, as he well understood, are ever as dear to the grandmother as to the mother.

Henry Clay, the pride and honor of his country, always expressed feelings of profound affection and veneration for his mother. A habitual correspondence and enduring affection subsisted between them to the last hour of life. Mr. Clay ever spoke of her as a model of maternal character and female excellence, and it is said that he never met his constituents in Woodford county, after her death, without some allusion to her, which deeply affected both him and his audience. And nearly the last words uttered by this great statesman, when he came to die, were, "Mother, mother, mother." It is natural for us to feel that she must have been a good mother, that was loved and so dutifully served by such a boy, and that neither could have been wanting in rare virtues.

If each mother, according to her several ability, seeks to develop the higher and better faculties of her children, the reward will be as great as the aim is noble.

Who has the mind or character in hand while it is yet so flexible and ductile that it can be turned in any direction, or formed in any shape? It is the mother. From her own nature, and the nature of her child, it results that its first impressions must be taken from her. And she has every advantage for discharging the duty. She is always with her child—if she is where mothers ought to be—sees continually the workings of faculties; where they need to be restrained, and where led and attracted. Early as she may begin her task, let her be assured, that her labor will not be lost because undertaken too soon. Mind, from the first hour of its existence, is ever acting; and soon may a mother see that, carefully as she may study her child, *quite as carefully is her child studying her.* Let her watch the varying expression of its speaking face, as its eyes follow her, and she will perceive its mind is imbibing impressions from everything it sees her do; and thus showing, that, before the lips have begun to utter words, the mind has begun to act, and to form a character. Let her watch on; and when, under her care, the expanding faculties have begun to display themselves in the sportiveness of play, how often will she be surprised to find the elements of character already fixed, when she has least expected it. She has but to watch, and she will find the embryo tyrant or philanthropist, warrior or peace-maker, with her in her nursery; and then, if ever, her constant prayer should be, "How shall I order the child, and what shall I do unto him?" For, what he is to be, and what he is to do, in any of these characters, she must now decide. It is a law of our being that makes it so; a law that I could wish were written on every mother's heart by the finger of God, and on the walls of her nursery in letters of gold, that the mind of childhood is like wax to receive, but like marble to hold, every impression made upon it, be it for good or for evil. Let her then improve her power as she ought, "being steadfast, unmovable, always abounding in the work" which God requires at her hands; and let her know that her labor is not in vain in the Lord. For, even though her own eyes may not be privileged to witness in her child all that is noble and great and good, she may at least save him when her course on earth is finished. It is no picture of the imagination that I hold out, when I ask you to come and see the son of a faithful mother, who has long pursued his course of crime, till he seems hardened against everything good or true; yea, at times "sits in the seat of the scorner," and scoffs at everything holy and good—but yet hardened and dead as his heart may seem, as to everything else you may urge, there is one point on which, till his dying day, he can be made to feel. You touch it when you remind him of what he saw and felt when a child under the care of a tender mother. His sensibilities there he never utterly loses; and often, often, by that, as the last cord which holds him from utter perdition, is the prodigal drawn back and restored; so that, though "dead, he is alive again," though once "lost, he is found."

Such are some of the illustrations of a mother's power to do good to those most dear to her, and of the responsibility that springs from it. There is no influence so powerful as hers on the coming destinies of the church and the world. She acts a part in forming the ministers of religion and the rulers of the land, without which all subsequent training is comparatively vain. And to her, also, it falls to train those who are to be mothers when she is gone, and to do for their generation what she has done for hers.

Honor the dear old mother. Time has scattered the snowy flakes on her brow, plowed deep furrows on her cheeks, but is she not sweet and beautiful now? The lips are thin and shrunken, but those are the lips which have kissed many a hot tear from the childish cheeks, and they are the sweetest lips in all the world. The eye is dim, yet it glows with the soft radiance of holy love which can never fade. Ah, yes, she is a dear old mother. The sands of life are nearly run out, but feeble as she is, she will go further and reach down lower for you than any other upon earth. You cannot walk into a midnight where she cannot see you; you cannot enter a prison whose bars will keep her out; you can never mount a scaffold too high for her to reach that she may kiss and bless you in evidence of her deathless love. When the world shall despise and forsake you, when it leaves you by the wayside to die unnoticed, the dear old mother will gather you in her feeble arms and carry you home and tell you of all your virtues until you almost forget that your soul is disfigured by vices. Love her tenderly and cheer her declining years with holy devotion.

XV.

TIRED MOTHERS.

A LITTLE elbow leans upon your knee—
    Your tired knee that has so much to bear—
A child's dear eyes are looking lovingly
    From underneath a thatch of tangled hair.
Perhaps you do not heed the velvet touch
    Of warm, moist fingers holding you so tight;
You do not prize the blessing overmuch—
    You almost are too tired to pray to-night.

But it is blessedness ! A year ago
    I did not see it as I do to-day—
We are all so dull and thankless, and too slow
    To catch the sunshine till it slips away.
And now it seems surpassing strange to me
    That while I wore the badge of motherhood
I did not kiss more oft and tenderly
    The little child that brought me only good.

And if, some night, when you sit down to rest,
    You miss the elbow from your tired knee;
This restless curly head from off your breast;
    This lisping tongue that chatters constantly;

If from your own the dimpled hands had slipped,
    And ne'er would nestle in your palm again;
If the white feet into the grave had tripped—
    I could not blame you for your heartache then.

I wonder so that mothers ever fret
    At their little children clinging to their gowns;
Or that the foot-prints, when the day is wet,
    Are ever black enough to make them frown!
If I could find a little muddy boot,
    Or cap, or jacket, on my chamber floor—
If I could kiss a rosy, restless foot,
    And hear it patter in my house once more;

If I could mend a broken cart to-day,
    To-morrow make a kite to reach the sky—
There is no woman in God's world could say
    She was more blissfully content than I!
But, ah, the dainty pillow next mine own
    Is never rumpled by a shining head,
My singing birdling from its nest has flown—
    The little boy I used to kiss—is dead!

XVI.

RESPONSIBILITY OF PARENTS.

THERE is, perhaps, no duty more frequently inculcated and enjoined in the Bible, than that conveyed to the mind and understanding by the three words which we have placed at the head of this chapter. The family is of divine origin—instituted by Jehovah himself. He saw that it was not good that man should be alone, and created woman full of tenderness and love, blooming with beauty, and blushing with charms, without whom man, even in Paradise, could not be completely happy. The mutual desire of each for the other was fully realized in that union which of the twain made one flesh. It was required of them to obey their Heavenly Father, as it is of their offspring that they obey their earthly parents.

The spirit of disobedience soon manifested itself in the first human pair, and was transmitted to their children and to their children's children, and will continue down to the latest posterity. Notwithstanding this, however, the command of God is to all children, "obey your parents;" and the command of parents, is "bring up your children in the nurture and admonition of the Lord." This is no less imperative than that given to children. In the parents is placed the authority to educate, instruct, and train their children. And to the children it is said, "obey your parents in all things, for this is right and well-pleasing to the Lord."

Young parent, do you think that your children are yours, to have and to hold for your own pleasure and profit?—that you have *a right* to do what you will with them? You mistake; they are but LENT to you. Every child is but a sacred trust—a responsibility, than which there is none more mighty or fearful in life. "Train up this child for Me. I will require him at thy hands," says our Maker to every parent who receives a child. Judging by the declaration of inspiration, "Train up a child in the way he should go, and when he is old he will not depart from it," how many of our present men and women were trained up in that way; and what kind of an account will have to be given by their parents?

If you find an error in a child's mind, follow it up till he is rid of it. Repeat and fix attention on the exact error, until it can never be committed again. One clear and distinct idea is worth a world of misty ones. Time is of no consequence in comparison to the object. Give the child possession of one clear, distinct truth, and it becomes to him a center of light. In all your teaching—no matter what time it takes—never leave your pupil till you know he has in his mind your exact thought. In all explanations to your child,—and you will find innumerable explanations called for,—be patient and considerate, and leave no sense of vagueness behind, neither a repressive influence.

Children are more easily led to be good by examples of loving kindness, and tales of well-doing in others, than threatened into obedience by records of sin, crime and punishment. Then on the infant mind impress sincerity, truth, honesty, benevolence and their kindred virtues, and the welfare of your child will be insured not only during this life, but the life to come. Oh, what a responsibility to form a creature, the frailest and feeblest that heaven has made, into the intelligent and fearless sovereign of the whole animated creation, the interpreter and adorer and almost the representative of Divinity—to train the ignorance and weakness of infancy into all the virtue and power and wisdom of mature years!

Give children a sound moral and literary education—useful learning for sails, and integrity for ballast—set them afloat upon the sea of life, and their voyage will be prosperous in the best sense of the word.

The child is no more dependent on his parents for his food and raiment, than for intellectual and religious nurture. If the former two be withheld, the little one soon perishes. If these be duly administered, and mental and religious culture be withholden, the child grows up to bodily maturity with strong animal passions and desires, and being goaded on by these, knows nothing of the restraints felt by one who has been carefully trained and instructed in the things spiritual, as well as provided for in things temporal, and consequently is fit for little else than the doing of what should be left undone—and thus incurring the penalty of broken law. Better, far better for both parent and child, had the little one not been born, than that he should have a birth only that his body may be nourished to the stature of manhood.

This responsibility is as binding upon the father as upon the mother. The influence incidental to the marital and parental state cannot be delegated, husband to wife or wife to husband. The influences of each may affect different sides of the child-nature, but they must be united in force and good intention, else unfortunate and one-sided training will be the result.

In the old Jewish parental economy the father occupied a most important place; it was of Jehovah's ordination, and though time and a "long promised fulfillment" have modified some of its sterner conditions, it still remains the grand model.

Sentimental writers of the present day seem to unite in ascribing all holy and abiding influences to the tender ministrations of the mother. If this view be the correct one, it is unfortunate for at least two reasons; first, it places altogether too heavy a burden upon the mother, and, secondly, it would leave the offspring unstamped by the current individuality and personality of the father. There is something sweet and reverential in ascribing an abiding and holy aspiration to the anxious mother who has so often bended over our slumbering couches in tender and wondering solicitude. But if a mother with her manifold duties can do so much, how very much more could a mother *and* a father do? Responsibility rests upon each with equal weight, and to right-minded parents the loving burden is cheerfully and mutually borne.

By a curious, though well understood law, the father's influence is more directly recognized and appreciated by the daughter; while the son is more amenable to the precept and daily walk of the mother. There exists in the hearts of most men a tender and loyal chivalry for women. There abides in the imagination a glorified ideal, surrounded by a halo of romance. These sons go forth into the noisy world, wrestling with and overcoming obstacles. They leave on record frequently the secrets of their success. Many unite in ascribing the first dawning incentive and lofty desire to the teachings of the mother; hence the world has come to regard the mother's influence as much more potential than that of the father.

It is unfortunate that this opinion should prevail, for it is not true, though fathers may be only too ready to take advantage of it and put the whole burden of moral and character-training on the mother. No father has any right to take advantage of this subterfuge. Let him look into his own heart and history, and he will see how much he owes (or might have owed) of his present success or attainments to the discriminating and executive foresight of *his* father. The son is affected by the precepts that fall from the lips of his father and the paternal example set before him. He may not be as ready to reverence this teaching and give it its proper meed of praise, but the effect is there notwithstanding. The father addresses the business, intellectual and ambitious side of the nature, while the mother appeals more to the spiritual and affectionate. This is a fact in nature, and shows that Providence designed co-ordinate influences on the part of the parents, in order to produce symmetrical development.

This union of parental influence is equally necessary in the case of the daughter. The positions in a measure seem reversed. The daughter has a greater reverence for and yields a more ready acquiescence to, the requests and commands of the father. Examined closely there is nothing wonderful in this. He treats her as he wants other men to treat her, and as he treated her mother. This presupposes no lack of sternness nor chastisement, if that should be necessary. She knows how much she owes to the judicious and watchful solicitude of the father. In her modesty and lack of public opportunity she may never tell the world of this, but it is treasured up in her heart, and by and by she will whisper it to her children.

Parents should never delegate their duties to others so long as they are able to perform them themselves. These duties, as ordained by nature, briefly stated, are to provide for the physical wants, develop the immortal natures, and give tone and wise direction to the minds of their children. As for the first, the providing of food and clothing, we need not say much. This is not a place for intermedling. Parents generally know what ought to be done, and in any event they know what they can do.

The religious or spiritual side of the child's nature is too largely left to the Sabbath-school teacher, whose work is generally conscientiously done so far as there is opportunity, and it is good as far as it goes. But the Sabbath-school is more a place for recitation than for moral and religious training; this latter should be done at home. "Train up a child in the way he should go and when he is *old* he will not depart from it." "My word shall not return unto me void." It is for us to sow the seed, God will send the dew, sunshine and rain. The skeptic may sneer and the indifferent turn aside carelessly from such sentiments, but all must admit, whether from personal experience or universal testimony, that no one has ever been the worse for sound and judicious religious training. Who shall measure what might be said affirmatively? The child of larger growth soon comes more or less under the influence of the minister, but the parental obligation is not discontinued by this fact, simply enlarged.

We send the children to school, and largely hold the teacher responsible for their mental progress. It is fortunate that, as a class, school teachers are conscientious, unselfish and painstaking, but after all what can they do, when we realize the number they have to teach and the limited time in which to do it? Their efforts must be largely expended in producing mechanical expertness in the various branches of modern learning. The impulse, incentive and fostering care *must* largely come from the parent. The minister and teacher may supplement your teaching, or they may rush in when you abandon your duty; but nature never intended that they should supersede you. You are the model. You are the guide.

For the want of the due exercise of parental authority multitudes of children of both sexes are growing up candidates for every evil work. How often have we seen the mother parley with her darling child at the table, for example:—There are pies, cakes, preserves, and the like upon the table, and plainer food also; the child, prompted by pampered appetite, asks for pie, perhaps; the mother says no—you must eat some of the coarser food first—the child says not so. After much effort to persuade, and not a little noise and clamor on the part of the dear little rebel, the mother yields—the child has conquered—and this same performance is gone through with every day, or as often as the temptation arises. What a fearful responsibility rests upon such parents—deliberately ruining their children,—making them wretched for this world, even to say nothing of that which is to come. No such child knows anything about obedience. If he ever does what he is told to do, it is from some other motive than that of obedience. Such a child will not be very likely to obey God, or regard man any farther than prompted by self-interest.

The main effort in this life with many seems to be to avoid responsibility. My friends, don't cheat yourselves; this cannot be done. If there is an eternity, somewhere in that eternity responsibility must be met. The responsibilities of life are tremendous. Reader, God has something for you to do, and which you can do better than any other being in the universe, or He would not have created you to do it, and somewhere in existence you will work out the problem of your destiny. This must be! God makes no mistakes; so don't shirk responsibility, for you cannot if you would. Face it like a man! and discharge it faithfully.

XVII.

AMUSEMENTS.

OLD boys have playthings as well as young ones; the difference is only in the price. The permission of lawful enjoyment is the surest method to prevent unlawful gratifications. Fun is worth more than physic, and whoever invents or discovers a new supply deserves the name of a public benefactor. A man cannot burrow in his counting-room for ten or twenty of the best years of his life, and come out as much of a man and as little of a mole as when he went in. Repose beautifies the heart and adorns the life. It is to labor what the shadow is to the sun. There is as much science in recreation as in labor. To a brisk bustling man, nothing makes time pass heavily but pastime. Mirth is short and transient, cheerfulness fixed and permanent.

"All work and no play makes Jack a dull boy;
All play and no work makes Jack a mere toy."

Most men that follow sports, make them a principal part of their life; not reflecting that while they are diverting themselves, they are throwing away time. We alter the very nature and design of recreation, when we make a business of it. He that follows his recreation instead of his business shall, in a little time, have no business to follow. Of all diversions of life, there is none so proper to fill up its empty spaces, as the reading of useful and entertaining authors; and with that the conversation of a well-chosen friend.

It has been assumed—and it is evidently a true position—that *inaction* is not the rest that re-invigorates the exhausted energies of either the mind or body, but a new direction of effort, by which new muscles of the body, or new faculties of the mind, are brought into activity. The true repose, then, which should follow every life-conflict—and they are of almost daily occurrence—is an entire diversion of the thoughts and feelings into some new channel. If this be not done, there can be no rest; for the current of thought will flow on unchecked, until the mind becomes diseased, and loses half its power.

And herein we see the use of amusements, or these innocent employments that divert the mind, and fill it with pleasing emotions. After the business of the day is over, these come in their natural order, to refresh and strengthen for new efforts; and it is more in accordance with the dictates of right reason to seek for re-invigoration in these than in dull inaction.

At all suitable times, young men will find it useful to seek for recreations and innocent amusements. It will give their minds a healthier tone, and bring them into associations different from business associations, by which they will be able to see new phases of character, and judge more kindly of their fellows. Amusements, therefore, we hold to be essential to the health of both body and mind. But, like every other good, they are liable to be perverted; and the young are more in danger of perverting them than those who have passed the prime of life. Nearly all the various amusements, public and private, that are entered into at this day, are innocent and useful in themselves, although some of them are sadly perverted to evil ends. When made a school of morals, the stage is a powerful teacher of truth, because it shows us vice or virtue in living personifications, but as it now is, we are compelled to acknowledge that it is a poor place of resort for the strengthening of virtuous principles.

From this brief presentation of the subject, every one must see that the views taken by those who inveigh against amusements, as either sinful or entirely useless, are erroneous, and founded upon false notions of man's moral nature. Our life here is for the development and perfection of our characters as immortal beings, created originally in true order, and afforded all possible means for a return to true order.

There are boys so circumstanced, as to be deprived of nearly all amusements at an age when work and play should each come in right order. These are apt to make men who have little sympathy for young people, and who regard all amusements as waste of time, and enervating to the character. They constantly refer back to their own uncheered boyhood as evidence that amusements are valueless; not thinking that the very aspect they show to the world is one of the strong arguments in favor of their balancing influence. From men of this class, as well as from religious ascetics, we have a steady warfare upon all amusements.

The true end of all amusement is, as we have seen, that recreation of the mind which will enable it the better to perform its useful tasks when the hour of duty returns. It should come up from them re-invigorated; and this can hardly be the case, if there should be in them anything that excites low, sensual, or impure emotions; or that insinuates false sentiments on any subject.

The effect of amusements on your state of mind will always indicate this utility or hurtfulness. If, after their enjoyment, you return to your regular duties, with a mind re-invigorated and cheerful, then they have done you good. But, if the usual things that demand your care and labor seem afterwards tame and irksome, and your thought wanders away from them to the evening's entertainments, then you may well question their good influence. Beware, in this case, how you let mere amusement and recreation make large demands on your leisure time; for you are in danger of being drawn away from that abiding interest in useful employments by which alone man rises in the scale of worldly prosperity, or becomes honorable and happy.

XVIII.

ASSOCIATIONS.

WASHINGTON was wont to say, "Be courteous to all, but intimate with few, and let those few be well tried before you give them your confidence." It should be the aim of young men to go into good society. We do not mean the rich, the proud and fashionable, but the society of the wise, the intelligent and good. Where you find men that know more than you do, and from whose conversation one can gain information, it is always safe to be found. It has broken down many a man by associating with the low and vulgar, where the ribald song and the indecent story were introduced to excite laughter and influence the bad passions. Lord Clarendon has attributed his success and happiness in life to associating with persons more learned and virtuous than himself. If you wish to be respected—if you desire happiness and not misery, we advise you to associate with the intelligent and good. Strive for mental excellence and strict integrity, and you never will be found in the sinks of pollution, and on the benches of retailers and gamblers. Once habituate yourself to a virtuous course—once secure a love of good society, and no punishment would be greater than by accident to be obliged for a half a day to associate with the low and vulgar.

Scarcely anything has a more decisive influence in forming the character and fixing the destiny of a young man for both worlds, than the company he keeps. It is a maxim of Divine wisdom, and it comes to you confirmed by the experience of all ages,—He that walketh with wise men shall be wise, but a companion of fools shall be destroyed. We have often wished that we had kept an account of the youths we have known to be ruined by this cause. The number is fearfully large; and of all who have to our knowledge been corrupted in their morals and blasted in their prospects for time and eternity, we can recollect very few whose career in vice and infamy could not be traced back to the influence of evil companions. Oh, how many apprentices and clerks and students and young professional men have we known utterly and forever ruined by the cause here referred to! Once of fair morals and bright prospects, the pride of fond parents and the hope of society, in an unguarded hour they were drawn into the society of unprincipled associates, went with them to the gaming-table, to the house of infamy, to the place of drinking, revelry, and profane mirth, and having thus broken away from the bonds of virtue, of decency, and self-respect, they found themselves as it were on enchanted ground, within the inextricable toils of the destroyer, and were drawn deeper and deeper in corruption and shame, till character gone, hope gone, all gone, they sunk, some into an untimely grave, victims of their vices, while others were obliged to quit their business and their prospects, and lived a grief and a sorrow to their parents and their friends. Oh that we could call up and place these unhappy persons before you, and let you see them in all their degradation and loss of hope for both worlds! Sure we are that, warned by their melancholy example and miserable end, you would thank us for this word of admonition, and shun, as you would the way of perdition, the society of the immoral and the vicious. Beware of the beginnings of evil. It is much easier to *avoid* bad company, than to break away from it when you are once within its bewildering, deadening influence. You may shun evil companions, if you please; but when you are linked in with them, you are committed to your fate, and no resolution will probably avail to break the connection or save you from the fatal consequences of its continuance.

Every young man may see how much depends upon his choice of associates. If he mingle with those who are governed by right principles, his own good purposes will be strengthened, and he will strengthen others in return. But if he mingle with those who make light of virtue, and revel in selfish and sensual indulgences, he will find his own respect for virtue growing weaker, and he will gradually become more and more in love with the grosser enjoyments of sense, that drag a man downward, instead of lifting him upward, and throw a mist of obscurity over all his moral perceptions.

It has been truly said, an author is known by his writings, a mother by her daughter, a fool by his words, and all men by their companions.

Intercourse with persons of decided virtue and excellence is of great importance in the formation of a good character. The force of example is powerful; we are creatures of imitation, and, by a necessary influence, our tempers and habits are very much formed on the model of those with whom we familiarly associate. Better be alone than in bad company. Evil communications corrupt good manners. Ill qualities are catching as well as diseases; and the mind is at least as much, if not a great deal more, liable to infection, than the body. Go with mean people, and you think life is mean.

It is rare that a novice in iniquity falls at once into the hands of finished seducers. Novices are usually reached at first by young men of their own age, who have recently taken their first degrees in glaring sin. The merry, roystering jollity of such sinners, their gayety of spirit, their apparent happiness, the glowing descriptions they give of their festivities, the sly hints they throw out at the *greenness* of the uninitiated, the half-playful, half-earnest banterings with which they greet their bashful excuses for not joining in their vices, are the first seductive influences which usually reach young men from the wicked. By these means they learn to love their society; they lose their relish for the purity and quiet of home; they feel mortified at their ignorance of iniquitous practices; until, surrendering themselves to the guidance of these children of sin, they take costly lessons for themselves in Sabbath-breaking, in drinking revels, and in forbidden visits to various places of amusement.

The power of example is proverbial. We are creatures of imitation, and nothing is of more importance to young men than the choice of their companions. If they select for their associates the intelligent, the virtuous, and the enterprising, great and most happy will be the effects on their own character and habits. With these living, breathing patterns of excellence before them, they can hardly fail to feel a disgust at everything that is low, unworthy, and vicious, and be inspired with a desire to advance in whatever is praiseworthy and good. It is needless to add, the opposite of all this is the certain consequence of intimacy with persons of bad habits and profligate lives.

Here, then, young man, is the turning-point of your destiny. When your heart first feels enchanted by young men whom you know to be the occasion of grief to their friends and suspicion to their employers, your danger is imminent and extreme. The fact that you fail to discern the full enormity of their practices, is the sign that you are marked for destruction.

Let every young man, then, seek for associations in life; but let him be exceedingly careful how he make his selection. Almost everything depends upon its being done with prudence.

Evil companions are, therefore, to be totally avoided. Safety is to be purchased only at the price of entire abstinence from their society; for, as he who tastes his first glass of intoxicating drink has no security against becoming a drunkard, so he who finds a little delight in the society of partially corrupted persons has abandoned the ground of absolute safety. He is within a charmed circle. The incantation has begun. The demon of the circle is nigh. Soon will he present the bond by which the young dupe will sign away his virtue, his hope, his soul. Beware! oh, beware, then, of every one of the seducers to vice! Reject the bad book; turn away from the vile picture; refuse your company to the wicked! Seek God and his children; so shall you happily escape the dangers of life, and win a crown of eternal glory!

The following beautiful allegory is translated from the German: Tophronius, a wise teacher, would not suffer even his grown-up sons and daughters to associate with those whose conduct was not pure and upright. "Dear father," said the gentle Eulalia to him one day, when he forbade her, in company with her brother, to visit the volatile Lucinda, "dear father, you must think us very childish, if you imagine that we should be exposed to danger by it." The father took in silence a dead coal from the hearth, and reached it to his daughter. "It will not burn you, my child;

take it." Eulalia did so, and behold! her delicate white hand was soiled and blackened, and as it chanced her white dress also. "We cannot be too careful in handling coals," said Eulalia, in vexation. "Yes, truly," said her father; "you see, my child, that coals, even if they do not burn, blacken. So it is with the company of the vicious."

No man can allow himself to associate, without prejudice, with the profane, the Sabbath-breakers, the drunken, and the licentious, for he lowers himself, without elevating them. The sweep is not made the less black by rubbing against the well-dressed and the clean, while they are inevitably defiled. The Persians have this beautiful fable to show the value of good company: "A philosopher was one day astonished by the fragrance of a piece of clay. On asking how it came to have so sweet a perfume, the clay answered: 'I was once a piece of common clay, but I was placed for some time in the company of a rose, and the sweet quality of my company was communicated to me; otherwise, I should only be a piece of common clay, as I appear to be.'" Tell me with whom thou art found, and I will tell thee whom thou art: let me know thy chosen employment, and what to expect from thee I know. Describe your company and you will describe yourself.

The awfully sad consequences of evil associations is exhibited in the history of almost all criminals. A young man, lately executed, made the following speech on the gallows: " This is a solemn day for me, boys! I hope this will be a warning to you against bad company—I hope it will be a lesson to all young people, and old as well as young, rich and poor. It was that that brought me here to-day to my last end, though I am innocent of the murder I am about to suffer for. Before my God I am innocent of the murder! I never committed this or any other murder. I know nothing of it. I am going to meet my Maker in a few minutes. May the Lord have mercy on my soul! Amen, amen." What a terrible warning his melancholy example affords to young men never to deviate from the straight line of duty. Live with the culpable, and you will be very likely to die with the criminal. Bad company is like a nail driven into a post, which after the first or second blow, may be drawn out with little difficulty; but being once driven in up to the head, the pinchers cannot take hold to draw it out, which can only be done by the destruction of the wood. Let you be ever so pure, you cannot associate with bad companions without falling into bad odor. Evil company is like tobacco smoke—you cannot be long in its presence without carrying away the taint of it. Tell us whom you choose and prefer as companions, and we certainly can tell who you are like. Do you love the society of the vulgar? Then you are already debased in your sentiments. Do you seek to be with the profane? in your heart you are like them. Are jesters and buffoons your choice friends? He who loves to laugh at folly is himself a fool. Do you love and seek the society of the wise and good? Is this your habit? Had you rather take the lowest seat among these than the highest seat among others? Then you have already learned to be good. You may not make very much progress, but even a good beginning is not to be despised. Hold on your way, and seek to be the companion of those that fear God. So you shall be wise for yourself, and wise for eternity.

XIX.

FRIENDSHIP.

FRIENDSHIP is a sweet attraction of the heart toward the merit we esteem or the perfections we admire, and produces a mutual inclination between two or more persons, to promote each other's interest, knowledge, virtue and happiness. The sweetest and most satisfactory connections in life are those formed between persons of congenial minds, equally linked together by the conformity of their virtues, and by all the ties of esteem. Friendship is the most sacred of all moral bonds. Trusts of confidence, without any express stipulation or caution, are yet, in the very nature of them, as sacred as if they were guarded with a thousand articles or conditions. Friendship has a notable effect upon all states and conditions. It relieves our cares, raises our hopes, and abates our fears. A friend who relates his success, talks himself into a new pleasure; and by opening his misfortunes, leaves part of them behind him. Friendship improves happiness, and abates misery, by the doubling of our joy and dividing our grief.

Friendship is a flower that blooms in all seasons; it may be seen flourishing on the snow-capped mountains of Northern Russia, as well as in more favored valleys of sunny Italy, everywhere cheering us by its exquisite and indescribable charms. No surveyed chart, no national boundary line, no rugged mountain or steep declining vale, put a limit to its growth. Wherever it is watered with the dews of kindness and affection, there you may be sure to find it. Allied in closest companionship with its twin sister, Charity, it enters the abode of sorrow and wretchedness, and causes happiness and peace. It knocks at the lonely and disconsolate heart; and speaks words of encouragement and joy. Its all-powerful influence hovers o'er contending armies, and unites the deadly foes in the closest bonds of sympathy and kindness. Its eternal and universal fragrance dispels every poisoned thought of envy, and purifies the mind with a holy and priceless contentment, which all the pomp and power of earth could not bestow. In vain do we look for this heavenly flower in the cold, calculating worldling; the poor, deluded wretch is dead to every feeling of its ennobling virtue. In vain do we look for it in the actions of the proud and aristocratic votaries of fashion; the love of self-display, and of the false and fleeting pleasures of the world, has banished it forever from their hearts. In vain do we look for it in the thoughtless and practical throng, who with loud laugh, and extended open hands, proclaim obedience to its laws—while at the same time the canker of malice and envy and detraction is enthroned in their hearts, and active on their tongues. Friendship, true friendship, can only be found to bloom in the soil of a noble and self-sacrificing heart; there it has a perennial summer, a never-ending season of felicity and joy to its happy possessor, casting a thousand rays of love and hope and peace to all around.

A man may have a thousand intimate acquaintances, and not a friend among them all. If you have one friend, think yourself happy. A friend—a real, true-hearted friend—is more rare than he should be. Why is it that selfishness predominates in the heart?—that he only is considered a friend who has money and influence? In the higher walks of life, how rarely is a true friend found—one who will act as he feels, and speak as he thinks. But among the humble and pure, you will occasionally find the germ of pure friendship. Ye who have found a true friend, appreciate his worth. If he labors to benefit you, say not a word, perform not an act, that will send a thrill of pain to his bosom. If there is a crime that betrays a vile heart, it is the wounding of pure affection. Many a one has seen too late the error of his course. When the grave has concealed his best friend, he felt—ah! words will not describe the feeling. Ye who are surrounded by the kind and good—the watchful and true-hearted—appreciate them, we pray you. Love them in return for their kindness, and to the close of life they will continue to guard and bless you. Never forsake a friend. When enemies gather around, when the world is dark and cheerless, is the time to try a true friend. They who turn from a scene of distress betray their hypocrisy, and prove that only interest moves them. If you have a friend who loves you, who has studied your interest and happiness, be sure to sustain him in adversity. Let him know that his former kindness is appreciated, and that his love was not thrown away. Real fidelity may be rare, but it exists in the heart. They only deny its worth who never loved a friend, or labored to make a friend happy.

Friends that are worth having are not made, but "grow," like Topsy in the novel. An old man gave this advice to his sons on his death-bed, "Never try to make a friend." Enemies come fast enough without cultivating the crop; and friends who are brought forward by hot-house expedients, are apt to wilt long before they are fairly ripened. "Friends are discovered rather than made," writes Mrs. Stowe. "There are people who are in their own nature friends, only they don't know each other; but certain things, like poetry, music and painting, are like the Freemason's sign—they reveal the initiated to each other."

There is no pre-eminence among true

friends; for whether they are equally accomplished or not, they are equally affected to each other. A false friend is like the shadow on the sun-dial, appearing in sunshine, but vanishing in shade.

A friend should be one in whose understanding and virtue we can equally confide, and whose opinion we can value at once for its justness and its sincerity. Relatives are not necessarily our best friends, but they cannot do us an injury without being enemies to themselves. A friend is often more valuable than a relative. Go to strangers for charity, acquaintances for advice, relatives for nothing. A friend of everybody is a friend to nobody.

When Socrates was asked why he had built for himself so small a house, he replied, "Small as it is, I wish I could fill it with friends." These, indeed, are all that a wise man would desire to assemble; for a crowd is not company, and faces are but a gallery of pictures, and talk but a tinkling cymbal, where there is no love. Without friends the world would be but a wilderness. It has ever been my opinion, says Horace, that a cheerful, good natured friend is so great a blessing, that it admits of no comparison but itself. Cicero used to say, that it was no less an evil for a man to be without a friend, than the heavens to be without a sun. It is not the seeing of one's friends, the having them within reach, the hearing of and from them, that makes them ours. Many a one has all that, and yet he has nothing. It is believing in them, the depending on them, assured that they are true and good to the core.

Old friends! What a multitude of deep and varied emotions are called forth from the soul by the utterance of these two words! What thronging memories of other days crowd the brain when they are spoken! Ah, there is a magic in the sound, and the spell which it creates is both sad and pleasing. As we sit by our fireside, while the winds are making wild melody without the walls of our cottage, and review the scenes of by-gone years which flit before us in swift succession, dim and shadowy as the recollection of a dream—how those "old familiar faces," will rise up and haunt our vision with their well remembered features. But ah, where are they? those friends of our youth—those kindred spirits who shared our joy and sorrows when first we started in the pilgrimage of life. Companions of our early days, they are endeared to us by many a tie, and we now look back through the vista of years, upon the hours of our communion, as upon green oases in a sandy waste. Years have passed over us with their buds and flowers, their fruits and snows; and where now are those "old familiar faces?" They are scattered, and over many of their last narrow homes, the thistle waves its lonely head; "after life's fitful fever, they sleep well." Some are buffeting the billows of Time's stormy sea in distant lands; though they are absent our thoughts are often with them. A few perhaps yet remain, and we meet them oft as we pursue our daily vocation. To those we cling with a closer grasp as the auburn of their locks fades into grey. They are as a cluster of sere leaves in winter which have withstood the chill winds of November; each one that drops off binds the others yet closer unto us. Time and changes cement our friendship, and when an old friend passes off the stage, his absence creates a blank which new ones can never fill. Our life is a devious path, and as our companions drop off one by one, and new faces supply their place, we seem to move in a strange world and amid strange people. The rocks and the hills, the streams and the trees remain in the places which they filled of yore, but the " old familiar faces" with whom we wandered along their banks and beneath their shade, have long since departed, and a sensation of loneliness comes over us, even when mingling in a crowd. The thoughts which fill the mind when musing upon the joys of "lang syne" are of a chastened character. We are freed for a time from the shackles of selfishness, and contemplate the purer and kindlier traits of the soul. We behold the footprints of Time as marked by the pencilings of decay—in the scenes of the past we behold a type of the future—the fate of our friends shadows forth that of ourselves, and dull are we if we rise not from fancied communication with old friends, both wiser and better men and women.

XX.

INFLUENCE.

INFLUENCE is the power we exert over others by our thoughts, words, and actions—by our lives, in short. It is a silent, a pervading, a magnetic, and a most wonderful thing. It works in inexplicable ways. We neither see nor hear it, yet, consciously or unconsciously, we exert it. No one can think, or speak, or act—no one can live—without influencing others. We all sometimes seem unconscious of this very important fact, and appear to have adopted the strange idea that what we do, or think, or say, can affect no one but ourselves. You influence others and mould their characters and destinies for time and for eternity far more extensively than you imagine. The whole truth in this matter might flatter you; it would certainly astonish you if you could once grasp it in its full proportions. It was a remark of Samuel J. Mills that "No young man should live in the nineteenth century without making his influence felt around the globe." At first thought that seems a heavy contract for any young man to take. As we come to apprehend more clearly the immutable laws of God's moral universe we find that this belting of the globe by his influence is just what every responsible being does—too often, alas, unconsciously. You have seen the telephone, that wonderful instrument which so accurately transmits the sound of the human voice so many miles. How true it is that all these wonderful modern inventions are only faint reflections of some grand and eternal law of the moral universe of God! God's great telephone—I say it reverently—is everywhere—filling earth and air and sea, and sending round the world with unerring accuracy, and for a blessing or a curse, every thought of your heart, every word that falls thoughtfully or thoughtlessly from your lips, and every act you do. It is time you awoke to the conviction that, whether you would have it so or not, your influence is world-wide for good or for evil. Which?

There is another immense fact which we

may as well look squarely in the face. *An influence never dies.* Once born it lives forever. In one of his lyrics, Longfellow beautifully illustrates this great truth:

> "I shot an arrow in the air,
> It fell to earth, I knew not where;
> *   *   *   *   *
> I breathed a song into the air,
> It fell on earth, I knew not where;
> *   *   *   *   *
> Long, long afterwards, in an oak
> I found the arrow, still unbroke;
> And the song, from beginning to end,
> I found again in the heart of a friend."

No thought, no word, no act of man ever dies. They are as immortal as his own soul. He will be sure to find them written somewhere. Somewhere in this world he will meet their fruits in part; somewhere in the future life he will meet their gathered harvest. It may, and it may not, be a pleasant one to look upon.

An influence not only lives forever, but it keeps on growing as long as it lives. There never comes a time when it reaches its maturity and when its growth is arrested. The influence which you start into life to-day in the family, the neighborhood, or the social circle, is perhaps very small now, very little cared for now; but it will roll forward through the ages, growing wider and deeper and stronger with every passing hour, and blighting or blessing as it rolls.

"Gather up my influence and bury it with me!" exclaimed a youth, whose unforgiven spirit was sinking into the invisible world. Idle request! Had he begged his friends to bind the free winds, to chain the wild waves, to grasp the fierce lightning, or make a path for the sand-blast, his wish would have been more feasible. The sceptical thought that fell as a seed of evil from the lip and grew in the heart of the listener into defiant infidelity, the light word that pierced the spirit like a poisoned dart, the angry glance which stirred the soul to anguish and made tears flow at the midnight hour, are all beyond our reach. The mind thus wounded sighs on, and after we are dead the chords vibrate which our fingers touched. The measure of that influence, for weal or woe, will lie hidden, a terrible secret, until the day when the spirit, blindly driven to despair and guilt, or blasted by sceptical thought, shall stand writhing and wretched to confront those by whom the offence came, and to teach that *influence is immutable and eternal.* It is *influence* that is thus powerful, not the influence of those in high stations. The effect of their conduct is more easily traced, because it works through public affairs. But the influence of a beggar girl is as potential in her sphere as is that of a queen in her more enlarged circle. Wealth, station, talent, may add to the force and extent of influence, but they cannot create it. It is an attribute of your nature, inseparable from it, inherent in it.

Your influence is not confined to yourselves, or to the scene of your immediate action; it extends to others, and will reach to succeeding ages. Future generations will feel the effects of your principles and your conduct. You are so connected with the immortal beings around you, and with those who are to come after you, that you cannot avoid exerting a most important influence over their character and final conditions; and thus, long after you shall be no more, nay, long after the world itself shall be no more, the consequences of your conduct to thousands of your fellow men, will be nothing less than everlasting destruction, or eternal life.

What if life is young, and its paths are strewed with flowers? What if the current of your ordinary ideas runs in a contrary direction? What if a due sense of the true responsibilities of life should restrain, in some degree, the gayety of your spirits? Are you, therefore, to trample upon the happiness of others? Are you to peril your own best interests? Remember, as is your influence, so is your destiny. There is a woe for those who suffer from evil influence; but a heavier, direr woe for them "by whom the offence cometh." Consider, therefore, my dear reader, with a seriousness worthy of your immortal nature, the bearings of this momentous question. Resolve, in the silent depths of your reflecting spirit, "I will take care of my influence!"

Among the many influences at work in our world it is noticeable that so many should be silent in their operations, and press on noiselessly and almost imperceptibly, and yet surely, toward completion. In the natural world around us how many of the causes which work for the good of man, blessing the earth and making it fruitful, are carried forward unassumingly, almost unnoticed save in their effect. The sunlight and the dew, the unceasing rotation of the seasons, and many other causes, which beautify or desolate the ground—how silently and beautifully carried forward, gently, like the soft breathings of an angel's lute, carrying hope and gladness to the hearts of men.

Where do we find truth in its mightiest power? Not surely in the breath of popular tumult or enthusiasm; not in the eloquent appeal or the marshalling of logic and argument, but in the deepest recesses of the fervent soul; in the unpretending life, and silent holy influence of him who strives to conform his life to its precepts. It is here that truth loves to dwell as a guardian spirit, to keep its charge from all impurity.

And in our hearts when attuned to holiness, would we but listen to their silent promptings, might we hear voices, soft as the echo of a seraph's murmur, blessing our souls with teachings of pure wisdom from the heavenly fount.

How much more powerful for good is the silent influence of a spotless example than the tumult of public life? The silent teachings of a life of purity, the fond expression of the soul's affection, the mild reproof from eyes of tenderness and love; what to these are the appeals of passion or argument—the fierce denunciation or passionate invective?

Let no one then despair of exerting influence, because the power is not his to mould listening senates to his will, or hold multitudes entranced in spell-bound wonder at the lightning of his eloquence, for a mightier and a more lasting power may be his in the exertion of the silent influence of sympathy and example. The storm and the thunder are needed at times, but not more than the sunlight and the dew; and in the hurry of our active life we should not forget the unassuming duties.

It is here, in the discharge of these duties, that woman shines in her greatest beauty. Unfitted for the stormy arena of public life, and for the use of outward power, it remains with her to win the hearts, and wielding but the weapons of sympathy and love, to rule the world. And her influence, more potent than war's horrid enginery, will be felt—will be obeyed. A whisper, a sigh, even a glance of love, will often reach the heart when the finest bursts of eloquence would be powerless, and the most conclusive arguments ineffectual.

Let us then be more mindful of these silent influences; for the pure heart radiates, as from the sun, rays of power, which insignificant as they seem, are to live and throb through all coming time.

XXI.

INTEMPERANCE.

THE bane of the American people is intemperance. The high and the low alike fall helplessly before it. It invades the pulpit, the bar, and the workshop; and many an otherwise happy fireside is turned into a sad abode of sorrow by this monstrous vice. It may seem incredible, but official facts show that more than sixty millions of dollars are annually spent in the city of New York alone for intoxicating drinks; while for the country at large the official report of the Bureau of Statistics shows the appalling sum of Five Hundred and Sixty Millions of dollars to be spent annually in this frightful way. The vigor of our nation is thus being destroyed; our alms-houses and prisons are filled; men who might be worthy are turned into hardened criminals or wrecks of insanity, brutalized in all their tastes and debased mentally and physically; homes are desolated, and misery and woe stalk abroad where otherwise there ought to be thrift and happiness.

Nor are the wives and mothers of our land exempt from the baleful influence of this fearful vice of intemperance. What so fearful a sight as a mother of children debased by rum? What a sad school of vice is that in which to rear a family, and how does the polluting influence spread to generations yet to come!

This vice is as old as the world's history. It is the product of no one nation or clime, but spreads its baneful influence over the whole earth, being no respecter of persons. The evils resulting from it are self-evident, and have been portrayed by eloquent tongues and pens, until the people have become more or less hardened and calloused to the direful truth. Its evil effects are felt in every town, county, state—indeed it has become a distinct National curse, and needs a National remedy.

To what causes may be attributed the prevalence of this curse? Are we by nature prone to its indulgence? Are its social surroundings irresistibly fascinating? Is it a habit or disease?

This question, of course, must be more or less distinctly settled before we can decide upon an efficacious remedy in any or all of the cases. That it is a disease in some cases must be admitted. A friend of the writer, about thirty years of age, a lawyer of excellent reputation, possessing a cultivated mind and a large warm heart, tells us that he is tempted sometimes, almost beyond his powers of endurance; that resistance is agony, and that he has but one remedy and that is to fly from the sight and fumes of alcohol. We know something of his early life and history; that he had been carefully and judiciously trained in an exceptional home, and by fond and wise parents; hence our surprise at a statement of this kind. Upon inquiry as to the source or cause of this appetite, he said it was inherited from his mother's family.

This is not an imaginary case; and permit us to add, that the longing had been resisted, and we believe, the victory fully won, all because of judicious moral and religious home training.

It is much easier to break up a habit than cure a disease, but in either case the scars are generally left behind.

In these days of enlightenment and agitation on this subject, there is no need for any one to allow this habit to creep upon him ignorantly. It is no easier to take the first glass than to tell the first lie. But after, what then? How many glasses shall succeed the first? Of course, it would be better never to take the first glass, and many more. But suppose you have, must you keep on? No! No! Stop at once. Ask yourself: "How much do I profit by this indulgence; how much pleasure do I derive from it; does or will it pay me in any way? I have made the mistake of getting into this business, but had I not better get out of it now? I can certainly do it much more easily than at a later period." Let every young man over whom this habit is gaining control, address himself with this self-enquiry, and see to it that he answers it practically.

The associations of young men frequently lead them into this habit. We are known by the company we keep. No matter what our morals or acquirements may be, we are bound to descend to the level of our associations. We cannot bring them up to our level, nor avoid the contamination of evil communications. This is a plain, common-sense view of the matter. It is without the fuss, and fury, lurid and sulphurous epithets, florid rhetoric abounding in so many treatises on this subject. But what is the use in stating as though it were some new fact, what is already so well known—indeed is self-evident? Let us glance at the temperance literature of the present day, and of past periods, and we shall find it lacking in dignity and common sense. No doubt many of these writers mean well, but they seem deficient in true wisdom and human experience.

It is about time a new departure was taken. The people are painfully interested, and earnestly anxious to be shown some way to cure this national moral illness. Merely to be told they are ill, and the nature of the disease, is not sufficient. The antidote is wanted and the knowledge to administer it.

This thought brings to our attention a somewhat delicate question, and one about which there is much skepticism and uncertainty; viz., National legal force, or in other words, Prohibition.

There are phases of this question that the real friends of reform should weigh most carefully before forming a definite conclusion; for this opinion once formed, becomes the basis of their future action. The ultimatum of the Prohibitionists in the various States is a stringent amendment to the various State constitutions, doing away entirely and forever with intoxicants as a beverage. This is a consummation devoutly to be desired; but can it be reached at once, or must the good end be attained by degrees? It is not enough to register a law on the statute books; it must also be indelibly pressed upon the hearts and consciences of the people, in order to insure its enforcement and prevent its becoming, like too many other good laws, simply a dead letter. We know a town containing eight thousand inhabitants that supports within its boundaries thirty-two whisky shops at an expenditure of six hundred and fifty dollars per day. Each one of these places is a center of influences that are ever growing and multiplying in an astonishing ratio. Each is made attractive in its way. The rising generation may daily see many of their associates, and, sad to say, their elders, who ought to set them a better example, entering these places of debauchery. It is only a question of time before these eddying circles draw them into this devouring maëlstrom. There is another blighting feature that we would be remiss in our duty did we not notice, and that is the corrupting and corroding political influence, that must, and does emanate from each of these places of sin. This whisky element is not confined to any one party, exclusively, though it always casts its vote solidly. Nominees to local or other offices are given to understand that they must, in some form or other, cater to this faction, if they would not sign their political death warrants.

It would not do, nor be correct, to say that the venders of alcoholic stimulants were of all men the most evil. We are acquainted with many among this class who possess warm hearts and generous impulses. They have drifted into this wretched business and believe it to be as legitimate as a thousand other callings. They are zealous in trying to protect what they are pleased to call their business interests, while their opponents are not equally in earnest in carrying out their convictions. Few give this subject attention specifically, until the evil enters their own homes—and then it may be too late.

There must be more consistency, better direction and consolidation of purpose on the part of the reformers, before they can reasonably expect to be successful in routing this well equipped and entrenched foe.

Each town has a remedy in its own hands, in the election of suitable excise commissioners. In the choosing of such, let the issue be to decrease the number of hotels to only so many as will suitably accommodate the traveling public, and see to it that the proper men shall have charge of these.

Then the places themselves will be made more respectable and there will be a less number of centers from whence radiate such destructive blights. This thing could be brought about in almost every town, and it would certainly be an elementary victory. The masses can more readily be brought to entertain and prosecute reforms than revolutions; and by following up each successive step in the right direction, quite as radical a change can ultimately be brought about, and, what is of more consequence, sustained.

The various temperance organizations, no matter how much they may differ in their rituals, ought to be a unit on the main question. They ought to assemble in mass convention and formulate their rallying cry. State committees should be formed with sub-committees in every district. The friends of this advance movement should be thoroughly organized with a view to ultimately control the Legislatures. But the reform to be thorough must be completely worked out in the various local centers, and thence proceed outward and combine for the general movement.

We are at war with alcohol in every form, and under every disguise; and this war we mean shall last while we last. We believe it to be the fatal foe to every precious interest in life here and hereafter. It destroys property, intellect and life. Why cannot its sad victims be made to pause one moment for calm reflection upon the certain and sad consequences of their evil habit? How can the nation be made to see it, and to rouse itself and shake off this deadly incubus? Will statistics wake the people? Here they are from official data. More than one hundred and twenty millions of dollars *more* are yearly spent in the United States for rum than the value of *all* the flour, cotton goods, boots and shoes, woolens, clothing, books and newspapers—more than the above *six* principal industries per year! You don't believe it? Well, it is true, nevertheless. This we know. But no pen can portray the deadly list of ills that follow in the train of this satanic sin; of hopes blighted; of intellects debased; of homes ruined; of hearts broken; of virtue lost; of children debauched in their young prime; of sorrow, misery and woe here, and heaven lost!

Reader, do you drink? Stop! right now! Break that glass at once and forever! Pause and turn your thoughts within for a little calm reflection. Are you a drunkard? Look upon that pale and wasted wife and mother, and at your sad home, and ask, "Did I cause this ruin?" Are you a moderate drinker? Remember there is *death* in that cup! Young man, beware of social influences! Have the courage to say No! so will you secure your own self-respect and the respect of those who have not your courage.

It is the moral ruin which is caused by rum which we wish we had the power to depict in all its sulphurous hues. The people would stand aghast with fright, and with one accord would say, "This thing must stop!" And it would stop; and in its stead we would have a nation of sober men; happy homes, filled with love; happy men, happy wives, happy mothers, happy children! What a leap forward will be gained, when virtue shall take the place of vice in every human heart; when every aspiration should be for something higher and nobler, than for something low and vile? Why not? Sure enough, why not?

XXII.

INDOLENCE.

IN the history of most successful men, whether in science, art, or trade, it will be found that the first real movement upwards did not take place, until, in a spirit of resolute self-denial, indolence, so natural to almost every one, was mastered. Necessity is, usually, the spur that sets the sluggish energies in motion. Poverty, therefore, is oftener a blessing to a young man than prosperity; for, while the one tends to stimulate his powers, the other inclines them to languor and disuse. But, is it not very discreditable for the young man, who is favored with education, friends, and all the outside advantages which could be desired as means to worldly success, to let those who stand in these respects, at the beginning, far below him, gradually approach as the steady years move on, and finally outstrip him in the race? It is not only discreditable, but disgraceful. A man's true position in society, is that which he achieves for himself—he is worth to the world no more, no less. As he builds for society in useful work, so he builds for himself. He is a man for what he does, not for what his father or his friends have done. If they have done well, and given him a position, the deeper the shame, if he sink down to a meaner level through self-indulgence and indolence.

Indolence destroys more than industry; and many a drone who has perished prematurely, had his friends been equally honest with Sir Horace Vere, would have had it said of him, as that nobleman said of his brother, when the Marquis of Spinola asked, "Pray, Sir Horace, of what did your brother die?"

"He died of having nothing to do!" was the bluff knight's reply.

Excellence is providentially placed beyond the reach of indolence that success may be the reward of industry, and that idleness may be punished with obscurity and disgrace.

A lazy boy makes a lazy man just as sure as a crooked sapling makes a crooked tree.

Think of that, my little lads. Who ever saw a boy grow up in idleness that did not make a lazy, shiftless vagabond when he was old enough to be a man, though he was not a man in character, unless he had a fortune left him to keep up appearance? Those who make our great and useful men were trained in their boyhood to be industrious.

To a young man who has acquired the habit of indulging himself in morning slothfulness, it will be something of a trial to rise at five o'clock, in both winter and summer; but the self-denial practiced in doing this will be so fully repaid, in a little while, that we are sure no one, who has awakened up to the responsibility of his position, and the incalculable benefits that must result from efforts such as he is making, will sink down again into disgraceful indolence.

Laziness grows on people; it begins in cobwebs and ends in iron chains. The more business a man has to do the more he is able to accomplish, for he learns to economize his time. "I can't find bread for my family," said a lazy fellow in company. "Nor I," replied an industrious miller; "I am obliged to work for it."

Activity is the result of some end or affection of the mind. Where no purpose is in the mind there is indolence; but when there is an end in view of sufficient importance, all the powers of the mind come into spontaneous activity. Now, will any young man say that there are not objects for him to attain, of sufficient importance to awaken him from his habits of indolence, no matter how much he have confirmed himself in them? We know there is not one who does not, at times, feel the necessity of concentrating every energy he possesses upon the accomplishment of some end; but the evil is, the thoughts are not kept steadily fixed upon the end, but are allowed to wander off to sport with unimportant things, or to retire in mere idle musings; and thence comes indolence; for if there is no purpose, there will be no activity.

An active and energetic mind may achieve much, even where there is great want of order; but indolence chains a man down, and keeps him fast in one position; it is, therefore, the most serious defect of the two, and should be striven against with unwearying perseverance.

Self-complacency begets indolence, a condition alike disastrous to nations and to individuals. Indolence, poverty; poverty, misery. Indolence imparts vice; vice leads to crimes, and crimes to the gallows.

It is an error to believe that the vehement passions alone, like love or ambition, triumph over the rest. Indolence, nerveless as it may be, is generally master of every other; it steals dominion over every action of life, and stealthily paralyzes alike all passions and all virtues.

Indolence leaves the door of the soul unlocked, and thieves and robbers go in and spoil it of its treasures.

XXIII.

INTEGRITY.

IF it be admitted that strict integrity is not always the shortest way to success, is it not the surest, the happiest, and the best? A young man of thorough integrity may, it is true, find it difficult, in the midst of dishonest competitors and rivals, to start in his business or profession; but how long ere he will surmount every difficulty, draw around him patrons and friends, and rise in the confidence and support of all who know him?

Look around over your community, and see who they are that are most prospered in their temporal interests, happiest in their lives, and most respected in their characters. Are they not the men of firm and decided principles,—of fair and open conduct? There are, thank God, many such in the midst of us; many, who know not how to sacrifice their conscience to their interest,—many who conduct their affairs with strict probity, with a noble, unbending regard to truth and duty. Are not these the characters whom you and all men most respect and esteem? Are they not in the greatest credit and in the happiest condition, sharing largest in the pleasures of an approving mind, and in the confidence and love of their fellow men? Let these men be your pattern; tread in their steps, imitate their virtues, and rise to their honor and happiness. What, if in pursuing this course, you should not, at the close of life, have so much money by a few hundred dollars? Will not a fair character, an approving conscience, and an approving God, be an abundant compensation for this little deficiency of pelf?

One of the first effects of integrity is to secure to its possessor the *confidence* of society. To have the confidence of others, is to have influence over them, for men readily yield themselves to the guidance of those in whom they confide. Hence, a reputation for lofty integrity is a better capital than gold;—it is more persuasive than eloquence;—it is more powerful than the sword. A remarkable example of its influence is furnished in the rivalry of Robespierre and Mirabeau, during the first epochs of the French Revolution.

A character for integrity, accuracy, and promptness acquired while learning any branch of business is the best capital which a young man can have. It will make him friends, open before him doors of enterprise, and set him forward in the world with every facility of prosperity and success. I have mentioned a character of integrity, by which I mean a character of high moral principle; of unbending uprightness and honor; it is worth everything to a young man, and he should guard it as his richest treasure, even as his life's blood. It is indeed his life in all that relates to his happiness and success in the world. It is a crown of gold to him now, and preserved untarnished in the fear and love of God, it is a pledge of a crown of glory reserved for him in heaven.

Cultivate the loftiest integrity, even in connection with the smallest matters. Are you a clerk? See to it that your minutest entries are strictly correct; that you never appropriate one cent of your employer's money or property to your own uses. Deal with honorable exactness toward all who trade at your store or counting-room. Eschew all *business lies*, in selling goods. If, in measuring or weighing an article, you discern defects which lessen its value, boldly make them known. Do not permit a dishonest employer to compel you to be his instrument,—his tool for doing wrong. Let him distinctly understand that *you* do not hesitate between dishonor and dismissal. Prove, if need be, by the loss of your situation, that you prefer an honest crust to a dishonest banquet. If you are a mechanic, a farmer, or an artist, prosecute your daily tasks with the same careful diligence, in the absence, as in the presence, of your employer; thus proving that you are "*no eye-servant*," no mere "*man-pleaser*," but a conscientious and dignified young man; doing right, not for reputation's sake, but because you love it, and from a sense of obligation to Almighty God.

XXIV.

GENIUS.

GENIUS is that quality or character of the mind which is inventive, or generates; which gives to the world new ideas in science, art, literature, morals, or religion; which recognizes no set rules or principles, but is a law unto itself, and rejoices in its own originality; which admitting of a direction, never follows the old beaten track, but strikes out for a new course; which has no fears of public opinion, nor leans upon public favor—always leads but never follows, which admits no truth unless convinced by experiment, reflection, or investigation, and never bows to the *ipse dixit* of any man, or society, or creed.

It is not the result of constant and unwearied labor. It cannot be acquired by the most stupendous efforts. It is Heaven-given. A man thus endowed and singled out from the mass of his fellowmen may not differ from them so much in appearance and action, yet he bears a spirit within him so susceptible to pain and pleasure, that what another would scarcely notice wounds his sensitive heart most deeply.

But he is keenly alive to all that is beautiful, and receives sensations of pleasure from objects which others would pass with indifference. His soul is like an Æolian harp, and every breath of heaven which touches its fragile strings makes richest melody.

It is only contact with the world and the rough blasts of daily life which wring forth such painful discord.

Thus it frequently happens that the men we are discussing appear to the world peculiar; but Longfellow has briefly but beautifully explained the cause in the following words: "Men of genius are often dull and inert in society; as the blazing meteor, when it descends to the earth, is but a stone."

From the realm of history genius takes periods that otherwise were dull and unsatisfactory, and casts around them such a fascination that they become familiar, and a charmed feeling is given which makes them always attractive; facts and legends are secured from the dusty archives of the past; and genius lights them with its transforming hues, pouring upon them its perfumed oil which feeds a blazing flame, unextinguished by the storms of ages.

Again, genius touches the unfinished picture, and instead of the dull and lifeless object which hung there before, the canvas seems inspired and the form is breathing—it speaks —it lives.

In the gorgeous piece of tapestry, woven in the silent loom of ages by hands that wrought unseen, and which sought to leave some golden links of memory between them and oblivion, the threads of genius shine forth conspicuous, and its strands run bright and silvery.

This cloth, quaintly wrought—curiously colored—but the moths of time have worked upon it, and when the baser fabric falls to fragments, the threads of genius will be still as beautiful and brilliant as ever.

It is one of the mysteries of our life that genius, that noblest gift of God to man, is nourished by poverty. Its greatest works have been achieved by the sorrowing ones of the world in tears and despair. Not in the brilliant saloon, furnished with every comfort and elegance; not in the library well fitted, softly carpeted, and looking out upon a smooth, green lawn, or a broad expanse of scenery; not in ease and competence—is genius born and nurtured; more frequently in adversity and destitution, amidst the harassing cares of a straitened household, in bare and fireless garrets, with the noise of squalid children, in the midst of the turbulence of domestic contentions, and in the deep gloom of uncheered despair, is genius born and reared. This is its birth-place, and in scenes like these, unpropitious, repulsive, wretched, have men labored, studied and trained themselves, until they have at last emanated out of the gloom of that obscurity the shining lights of their times; become the companions of kings, the guides and teachers of their kind, and exercise an influence upon the thought of the world amounting to a species of intellectual legislation.

Cleverness skims like a swallow in the summer evening, with a sharp shrill note, and a sudden turning. The man of genius dwells with men and with nature; the man of talent in his study; but the clever man dances here, there and everywhere, like a butterfly in a hurricane, striking everything and enjoying nothing, but too light to be dashed to pieces. The man of talent will attack theories, the clever man will assail the individual, and slander private character. But the man of genius despises both; he heeds none, he fears none; he lives in himself, shrouded in the consciousness of his own strength; he interferes with none, and walks forth an example that "eagles fly alone—they are but sheep that herd together." It is true, that should a poisonous worm cross his path, he may tread it under his foot; should a cur snarl at him, he may chastise it; but he will not, cannot, attack the privacy of another. Clever men write *verses*, men of *talent* write *prose*, but the man of *genius* writes *poetry*.

Genius, says Irving, seems to delight in hatching its offspring in by-corners. The house where Shakespeare was born was a small, mean-looking edifice of wood and plaster, and, according to tradition, he was brought up to his father's craft of wool-combing.

Hath God given you genius and learning?

It was not that you might amuse or deck yourself with it, and kindle a blaze which should only serve to attract and dazzle the eyes of men. It was intended to be the means of leading both yourself and them to the father of lights.

The drafts which true genius draws upon posterity, although they may not always be honored as soon as they are due, are sure to be paid with compound interest in the end.

The great and decisive test for genius is, that it calls forth power in the souls of others. It not merely gives knowledge but breathes energy.

XXV.

AMBITION VS. VANITY.

THE distinction is important. Of the first it is impossible to have too much; of the second we cannot have too little.

Ambition, proper, is so closely allied to self-respect, that it will not allow its possessor to commit a base or mean action. Ambition urges us to distinguish ourselves above the crowd of the idle and variable, by our industry, perseverance and constancy; and goads us on to win applause by our goodness and consequent greatness. It is a defensive armor which wards off the darts of the insidious and envious, who would bring us to a lower moral level than reason or conscience approves; incased in this armor we may walk among the haunts of vice without being contaminated. Without a due proportion of approbativeness a man cannot arrive at distinction, or leave behind him a name which the world holds in honor. It is the nurse of emulation, and becomes, when properly excited, the incentive or spur that urges us to perform great deeds. This element of character is as becoming to the humble as to the lofty in station. It is independent of rank, wealth or station, and best finds its utterance in the poetical song of Robert Burns, "A man's a man for a' that." Let every one become imbued with the sentiments expressed in this lyric, then he may become—though toiling all day and far into the night for scanty bread, being insecurely protected from the biting frosts or the rough blasts of heaven—an example to his kind and a blessing to himself and posterity.

Vanity, on the other hand, shows the little mind. It is the pride of externals and the fortunate position in which a man may be placed, and not of the qualities of the man himself. It assumes various offensive forms, and is, in all, a proof of ignorance and presumption. To the man of sense it is always ridiculous, and excites not his anger but his contempt. When we see a man vain of his high lineage, and expecting us to bow down to him because of the virtues of his ancestors, we despise him all the more for his high birth and the lack of true dignity with which he fills it. Proud men of this class have been happily compared to turnips and potatoes— all the best part of them is underground.

Equally offensive is the pride of wealth. This species of vanity is productive of much meanness. When we see a man vain in this direction we may be quite sure that he has gained his money in a dirty manner, and is equally ready to make a dirty use of it. If he have a large house, fine carriages and liveried servants, it is rather for ostentation than use. If he give charity, it is that it may be trumpeted abroad. He will refuse a pittance to the deserving object, if the gift is to remain a secret, when he would give a hundred to a less deserving one if the fact could be noised from the housetops. Such a man is not proud of being charitable, but of being thought so.

Again, we are vain of our beauty, strength, skill and talent.

When a woman is proud of her beauty, and

has neither wit, sense nor good nature, it is offensive. When a man boasts of his skill, in any particular pursuit, and thrusts it inopportunely forward, it is offensive: and when a man who has gained some credit for talent is apparently fearful that he will lose it, unless he daily impresses the recollection of it upon those about him, it is offensive.

There is too much "posing" for effect.

A thoughtful student of human nature says that vanity is the ruling passion of life. Perhaps more action may have its source in this, as a motive power, than in any other element of our nature. What we do or leave undone is too much affected by what we imagine some one will think or say. A friend of the author, cultured and of moderate means, possessed a cloak, comfortable, though somewhat soiled, and the question arose as to whether he should wear it the winter out or get a new one. In speaking of the matter afterward he said: "I imagined every one was looking at the seams and threadbare places, though I discovered no difference in the treatment I received from others; and I finally concluded that people paid much less attention to what I had on than I had supposed. The discovery was not without its influence."

The great Teacher, Christ Himself, who read all hearts and plumbed human nature to its lowest depths, spoke in no uncertain language, respecting this subject. "Without, ye are as painted sepulchres, beautiful to behold, but within loathsome corruption—dead men's bones." "I thank God I am not as other men are," with its contrast, "Lord, be merciful to me a sinner!" "Pray not to be seen of men." "Let not your left hand know what your right hand doeth."

The lesson of which the words just used were the text, was not only addressed to those of that day and age of the world, but to us and all succeeding generations.

This vanity is a disease that eats like a canker at the root of our moral well-being. It is the parent of envy and hypocrisy. In a nature predominated by this passion, there can be no room for modesty nor humility. Even the very sanctuary is polluted by its presence—the pure in heart, and those who would abide with God continually, are often pained by the pride and ostentation displayed in the temple where His honor loveth to dwell.

The child prattling at its mother's knee, and who ought to be sheltered in her loving bosom at this vital period of its life, when the nature is so plastic, is frequently paraded before the gaze of the gaping public, to feed the parents' morbid desire for praise. But what of the future of the child in whom the disease of vanity is thus early sown?

There are other kinds of vanity as offensive as those already mentioned. We would note especially that quality denominated sensitive pride, or the "pride that apes humility." It is founded not upon self-respect, but upon inordinate vanity, linked with some degree of cowardice. If lodged within the heart of a poor man or one of humble station in society, it leads him to imagine insults from the rich and lofty, which are never intended, and to suppose all the world is showing him disrespect, when in reality it is paying no attention to his existence. In the rich and powerful, it generally springs from some defect, physical or moral, as, for instance, in the case of Lord Byron and his lameness. So sensitive was he on this point, that he frequently cursed the mother who bore him, for bringing into the world a being so physically deformed.

Of the pride that apes humility, it may truly be said that it is, of all kinds of vanity, the most offensive. It is always tinctured with hypocrisy. The former may disgust us, but the latter morally offends.

The pride of wealth, rank, power, beauty or talent, though they may be unjustifiable, at least rest upon a basis that exists, or is supposed to exist; but the pride that imitates humility rests upon a lie, and thus becomes doubly offensive.

XXVI.

TACT.

A MAN of tact immediately fills a new position with naturalness, and, however he himself may feel its embarrassment, he forces the impression upon others, that he is just the man for the place. On the other hand, without tact, a man is impracticable. Change his occupation and he acts stiffly, awkwardly; he is like a stiff-jointed country recruit at his first drill; so uncouth are his movements, that lookers-on exclaim, "He will never do!" His friends lose their interest in his advancement. They fear to advance him, lest his clownishness should mortify their pride, and leave him to pine in the obscurity of a lowly position.

A recent English writer gives the following amusing off-handed portraiture of tact and talent. The writer recognizes the just distinction between these two qualities. Tact in its highest manifestation we have considered only a little short of absolute genius. Talent is something, but tact everything. Talent is serious, grave and respectable; tact is all that and more. It is not a sixth sense, but the life of all the five. It is the open eye, the quick ear, the judging taste, the keen smell, and the lively touch; it is the interpreter of all riddles—the surmounter of all difficulties—the remover of all obstacles. It is useful in all places and at all times; it is useful in solitude, for it shows a man his way through the world. Talent is power—tact is skill; talent is weight—tact is momentum; talent knows what to do—tact knows how to do it; talent makes a man respectable—tact will make a man respected; talent is wealth—tact is ready money. For all practical purposes of life, tact carries it against talent—ten to one. Talent makes the world wonder that it gets on no faster—tact excites astonishment that it gets on so fast; and the secret is that it has no weight to carry; it makes no false steps—it hits the right nail on the head—it loses no time—it takes all hints—and by keeping its eye on the weather-cock, is ready to take advantage of every wind that blows. It has the air of common-place, and all the force and powers of genius. It can change sides with hey-presto movement and be at all points of the compass, while talent is ponderously and learnedly shifting a single point. Talent calculates clearly, reasons logically, makes out a case as clear as daylight, utters its oracles with all the weight of justice and reason. Tact refutes without contradicting, puzzles the profound without profundity, and without wit outwits the wise. Setting them together on a race for popularity, pen in hand, and tact will distance talent by half the course. Talent brings to market that which is wanted; tact produces that which is wished for. Talent instructs; tact enlightens. Talent leads where no man follows; tact follows where humor leads. Talent is pleased that it ought to have succeeded; tact is delighted that it has succeeded. Talent toils for a posterity that will never repay it; tact throws away no pains, but catches the passion of the passing hour. Talent builds for eternity, tact on short lease, and gets good interest. Talent is certainly a very fine thing to talk about, a very good thing to be proud of, a very glorious eminence to look down from; but tact is useful, portable, applicable, always marketable; it is the talent of talents, the availableness of resources, the applicability of power, the eye of discrimination, the right hand of intellect.

But *tact* is the gift of nature! Yes! to some extent it is so. Versatility is easier to some than to others. That is, it requires less effort in some than in others, to adapt themselves to new relations to society. But even the versatility of the proudest sons of genius is the offspring of self-culture. The man who shines in an exalted position, who appears in it at such perfect ease that one might infer he was born to fill it, has gained the confidence which inspires him with ease by previous self-cultivation. A man who is true to himself is always in advance of his actual position; hence, when called to higher posts, he moves into them and fills them with propriety and dignity. This is *tact*. And the mental training which creates tact is within the reach of every young man.

XXVII.

COURAGE.

THERE are inner beauties of the soul, hidden resources of nature, and silent influences that remain unnoticed, save in their effects. But there is a quality or element of human character which always demands and receives attention. That quality is courage. Some contend that this quality is inherited or bestowed; others, that it is acquired. It displays itself in many directions, and is as varied in its manifestations as are the temperaments of the great multitudes of human units in whom it is ingrained.

It may be arranged under three heads, viz., physical, moral and mental.

By the first is understood that power or determination which enables us to face the cannon's mouth, or any other great danger to life and limb with determination and outward coolness.

Moral courage may be briefly defined as that quality of affection and conscience which enables us to boldly declare the truth under all circumstances; to keep ourselves unspotted from the world, and to die, if necessary, as martyrs for what is conceived to be some grand truth or underlying principle.

Of mental courage it may be said that it enables one who possesses it to undertake great enterprises, and to carry into action any conception of the mind.

Courage should be distinguished from foolhardiness. To be courageous one must realize the danger he faces. Armies may be recruited from the slums, and sacrificed as food for powder. But when a man seems singled out by fate, told to stand or run, and with no one standing behind, "about face," with steady nerve, we may be sure the hero stuff is in him.

We shall speak more particularly in this chapter of the necessity of possessing intellectual courage, and the advantages accruing.

Given this quality, a man may have his

heart's desire. Stumbling-blocks disappear from his path like the frost from the window pane before the morning sun. Draw the sword and throw away the scabbard. Do not leave open any road for retreat, when once the onward march has begun. Burn the bridges behind you. In the business of life, the way to fail is to think what you undertake is impossible of accomplishment. A ship on a storm-tossed shore sometimes flies into the very teeth of the storm to escape wreck.

Curs will fly from our path if they see we do not fear them. If we experience unforeseen difficulties, we must economize and work the harder. It is not dishonor to fail under impossibilities.

There are men in every community who are entitled to reputations for heroism. If they undertake any work or contract, their neighbors know it will be brought to a perfect conclusion. These men are living monuments not to a dead past. Their deeds are the inscriptions written in type so bold that "he who runs may read." These persons are held up as examples to a rising generation. They become models for imitation, and many who in their after lives attain to greatness and success, trace their first incentives for the higher and broader life, to such sources. They aspire to be to the young of their generation what these men have been to them. The good we do lives after us and is not interred with our bones.

What though we do sometimes stumble and fall; courage will set us on our feet again, and strengthen our hearts for the performance of greater efforts. Life is not a level plain, but a succession of hills and valleys. They rise before us on every hand, and in all matters of existence—in love, ambition, wealth, success or power; they are here, there—everywhere. Look about you and see who it is that succeeds. Not the timid ones who succumb to the first shadow which falls athwart their path; nor the man whose nerve will not keep his upper lip and jaw in place; not the man who gives up at the first trial. These men accomplish nothing. Success often sports with a man as a shy trout plays with the hook of an angler. Be wary, attend to regular business, and soon the nibble will end in a snapping bite.

Courage will fill our pockets with gold,

though that is not the chief end and aim of life. By it we rise to eminence. It will surround us with loving friends, who will not wait till life is ended to do us honor. Failure seems to be the rule rather that the exception. Too many approach the object of life and then recede, fearing to grasp it. Others fail because the way seems long and wearisome, and the path surrounded by too many difficulties. Surely this life is a school, and adversity is the schoolmaster.

We have an infinity of lessons to learn. We spread ourselves over too great a surface, thus frittering away many of our opportunities. If you cannot run up a hill, climb to the summit. The highway or by-path of life may be tedious to travel, but one made in the image and likeness of God should not tremble.

If you lack perseverance, have the determination to cultivate it. If you lack money, have the pluck to earn it. If you lack credit, be honest and show people that you deserve their confidence. If you are without position, don't be afraid to begin at the bottom of the ladder and work up. If you are wanting in firmness of character, keep away from temptation. "No" is a little word but terse and significant, be sure you utter it plain and distinct. Satisfy your own heart and self-respect, before looking about to see what others will think or say; they will come to your way of thinking by and by.

Let us not be fearful because we may have enemies; they are the spice of life and necessary to success—they are the long oars which in sturdy hands shoot the boat, deep though it be laden, far out and clear over the foaming breakers into a smooth sea beyond.

Many a swamp has stood sentinel to a land of promise beyond. Many a mountain has proved but a mirage. Life often ends in disappointment, but it can end happily. Let the dead bury its dead.

"Sorrow is frequently sent to make us purer—trouble to make us better—disappointment to increase our bravery."

Never despair. Your heart may be the cemetery of buried hopes—there is room yet for leafy-boughed success to spring from and around every grave, making the blessed future a labyrinth of fair bowers—a wilderness of joy—a heaven of heartfelt bliss.

XXVIII.

ECONOMY.

ECONOMY is a trite and forbidding theme. The young man will feel tempted to pass it by, and proceed to the next chapter. But we beseech him to read on, since his social advancement depends in a good degree upon his frugality. He had better be doomed, like the sons of ancient Jacob in Egypt, to make bricks without straw, than to enter the scenes of active life without economy for a companion.

The habit of spending money too freely in the gratification of a host of imaginary wants, is one into which young men of generous minds are too apt to fall. Limited to a small income previously, and compelled to deny themselves at nearly every point, they find it almost impossible to resist the impulse that prompts to self-gratification, and are thus led to spend, perhaps for years, the entire sum of their earnings, and, more than probable, to run into debt. The folly of this every one can see and acknowledge, and yet too many have not the resolution to act up to their convictions.

This habit of spending money uselessly has marred the fortunes of more young men than any other cause. It is a weakness that should be firmly and constantly resisted by every one. Money should be considered as a means by which man has power to act usefully in the world, and he ought to endeavor to obtain it with that end in view. The greater a man's wealth, the broader may be, if he but will it, the sphere of his usefulness.

Every man ought so to contrive as to live within his means. This practice is of the very essence of honesty. For if a man do not manage honestly to live within his own means, he must necessarily be living dishonestly upon the means of somebody else. Those who are careless about personal expenditure, and consider merely their own gratification, without regard for the comfort of others, generally find out the real uses of money when it is too late.

It is wiser and more honorable for a man to wear his coat three or six months longer, until he have the money with which to buy a new one, than it is to go in debt for the garment, and thus lay a tax upon his future income, or run the risk of not being able to pay for what he has worn, at the time agreed upon.

On every hand we see people living upon credit, putting off pay day till the last, making in the end some desperate effort, either by begging or borrowing, to scrape the money together, and then struggling on again, with the canker of care eating at their heart, to the inevitable goal of bankruptcy. If people would only make a push at the beginning, instead of the end, they would save themselves all this misery. The great secret of being solvent, and well-to-do, and comfortable, is to get ahead of your expenses. Eat and drink this month what you earned last month—not what you are going to earn next month. There are, no doubt, many persons so unfortunately situated that they can never accomplish this. No man can to a certainty guard against ill health; no man can insure himself a well-conducted, helpful family, or a permanent income. There will always be people who cannot help their misfortunes; but, as a rule, these unfortunates are far less trouble to society than those in a better position who bring their misfortunes upon themselves by deliberate recklessness and extravagances. You may help a poor, honest, struggling man to some purpose, but the utmost you can do for an unthrift is thrown away. You give him money you have earned by hard labor— he spends it in pleasure, which you have never permitted yourself to enjoy. Some people use one-half their ingenuity to get into debt, and the other half to avoid paying it. An old merchant gives this sound advice: "Never owe any more than you are able to pay, and allow no man to owe you any more than you are able to lose."

Credit never permits a man to know the real value of money, nor to have full control over his affairs. It presents all his expenses in the aggregate, and not in detail. Every one has more or less of the miser's love of money—of the actual gold pieces and the crisp bank notes. Now, if you have these things in your pocket, you see them, as you make your purchases, visibly diminishing under your eye. The lessening heap cries to you to stop. You would like to buy this, that, and the other; but you know exactly how much money you have left, and if you go on buying more things, your purse will soon be empty. You do not see this when you take credit. You give your orders freely, without thought or calculation; and when the day of payment comes, you find that you have overrun the constable.

Simple industry and thrift will go far toward making any person of ordinary working faculty comparatively independent in means. Even a working man may be so, provided he will carefully husband his resources, and watch the little outlets of useless expenditure. A penny is a very small matter, yet the comfort of thousands of families depends upon the proper spending and saving of pennies.

Mr. Spurgeon tells the following story of his early life: "When I was a very small boy, in pinafores, and went to a woman's school, it so happened that I wanted a slate-pencil, and had no money to buy it with. I was afraid of being scolded for losing my pencils so often, for I was a careless little fellow, and so did not care to ask at home; what, then, was I to do? There was a little shop in the place, where nuts, tops, cakes, and balls, were sold by old Mrs. Dearson; and sometimes I had seen boys and girls get trusted by the old lady. I argued with myself that Christmas was coming, and that somebody or other would be sure to give me a penny then, and perhaps even a whole silver sixpence. I would, therefore, go into debt for a slate-pencil, and be sure to pay at Christmas. I did not feel easy about it, but still I screwed my courage up, and went into the shop. One farthing was the amount; and as I had never owed anything before, my credit was good, the pencil was handed over by the kind dame, and I was in debt. It did not please me much, and I felt as if I had done wrong; but I little knew how soon I should smart for it. How my father came to hear of this little stroke of business I never knew, but some little bird or other whistled it to him, and he was very soon down upon me in right earnest. God bless him for it; he was a sensible man, and none of your children-spoilers; he did not intend to bring up his children to speculate, and play at what big rogues call financiering, and he therefore knocked my getting into debt on the head at once, and no mistake. He gave me a very powerful lecture upon getting into debt, and how like it was to stealing, and upon the way in which people were ruined by it; and how a boy who would owe a farthing might one day owe a hundred pounds, and get into prison, and bring his family to disgrace. It was a lecture, indeed; I think I can hear it now, and feel my ears tingling at the recollection of it. Then I marched off to the shop, like a deserter marched into barracks, crying bitterly all down the street, and feeling dreadfully ashamed, because I thought everybody knew that I was in debt. The farthing was paid amid many solemn warnings, and the poor debtor was set free, like a bird out of a cage. How sweet it felt to be out of debt! How did my little heart vow and declare that nothing should tempt me into debt again! It was a fine lesson, and I have never forgotten it."

The loose cash which many persons throw

away uselessly, and worse, would often form a basis of fortune and independence for life. These wasters are their own worst enemies, though generally found amongst the ranks of those who rail at the injustice of "the world." But if a man will not be his own friend, how can he expect that others will? Orderly men of moderate means have always something left in their pockets to help others ; whereas your prodigal and careless fellows who spend all, never find an opportunity for helping anybody. It is poor economy, however, to be a scrub. Narrow-mindedness in living and in dealing is generally short-sighted, and leads to failure. The penny soul, it is said, never came to two-pence. Generosity and liberality, like honesty, prove the best policy after all.

XXIX.

INDUSTRY.

MAN was made for action,—for duty and usefulness; and it is only when he lives in accordance with this great design of his being, that he attains his highest dignity and truest happiness. To make pleasure our ultimate aim is certainly to fail of it.

No matter what a young man's situation and prospects are; no matter if he is perfectly independent in his circumstances, and heir to millions; he will certainly become a worthless character, if he does not aim at something higher than his own selfish enjoyment; if he does not indeed devote himself to some honorable and useful calling.

I will add that so far as the formation of a good character and success in the world are concerned, I would rather have a child of mine begin life, with nothing to rely upon but his own exertions, than be heir to the richest estate in the country. Character and success depend vastly more on personal effort, than on any external advantages. With such effort, the humblest cannot fail to rise; without such effort, the highest cannot fail to sink.

A life of idleness is one of the direst of all curses. The doctrine that labor, even of the humblest character, is dishonorable, he must resolutely trample in the dust, as false and dangerous; and contend that an industrious, honest scavenger is really a more honorable man than the most fashionable dandy, who idles away his time on the pavements of Broadway, in ladies' drawing-rooms, in cafés, and in theatres. Thus, eschewing false ideas, and making every moment fruitful of some good to mind or body, to himself or to others, he cannot fail of a plenteous harvest of advantages as life advances.

Nothing great is ever achieved, except by industry and earnest application, combined with an orderly arrangement of all the means necessary to the accomplishment of the object in view. From this may be clearly seen the importance of habits of industry and order. Without them, little can be done ; with them, almost everything.

To be industrious, a young man must have a *useful pursuit* and a worthy aim. He must follow that pursuit diligently. Rising early and economizing his moments, he must earnestly persist in his toil, adding little by little to his capital stock of ideas, influence or wealth. He must learn to glory in his labor, be it mechanical, agricultural, or professional. He must impress himself deeply with the idea that a life of idleness is one of the direst of all curses.

Vast numbers of young men annually sink from positions of high promise into utter abandonment and destruction. But admit that the idle youth so trims between sloth and industry as to avoid utter ruin,—what then? He lives a useless, insignificant life. His place in society is aptly illustrated by certain books in a Boston library, which are lettered " Succedaneum " on their backs. " Succedaneum ! " exclaims the visitor ; " what sort of a book is that ? " Down it comes ; when lo ! a wooden block, shaped just like a book, is in his hands. Then he understands the meaning of the occult title to be, " In the place of another ;" and that the wooden book is used to fill vacant places, and keep genuine volumes from falling into confusion. Such is an idler in society. A man in form, but a block in fact.

As nothing great can be accomplished without industry and an earnest purpose, so nothing great can be accomplished without order. The one is indispensable to the other, and they go hand in hand, as co-workers, in man's elevation.

No young man should wish to live without work ; work is a blessing instead of a curse ; it makes men healthy, develops their powers of body and mind ; frees them from temptation, makes them virtuous and enterprising, and raises them to wealth, to honor, and to happiness. The working men of our country are its truest nobility. I refer of course both to those who work with their minds, and those who work with their hands ; and with these *workers* every young man should be prompt to enroll his name, and honor it, through life, by being a working man,—a producer, and not a mere consumer of what others earn. Having chosen his occupation, let him give himself to it with patient, untiring application—resolve to rise and to excel in it. If placed in discouraging circumstances, let him remember the adage of Cicero,—*Diligentia omnia vincit*. Many a dark morning has been succeeded by a long bright day. Our worthiest and best men have been formed amid difficulties and trials, and no young man should ever succumb to difficulties, or shrink from toil. Rightly met and borne they will give strength and firmness to his character, and so contribute to his higher and better success in life.

Martin Luther, Richard Baxter, John Wesley, Adam Clarke, Richard Watson, Napoleon Bonaparte, Elihu Burritt, and a host beside, might be quoted as demonstrations of what may be done by an industrious employment of moments during a life-time. But what does it avail to multiply examples? Let the young man resolve to become an example himself. Determine to make the most of your opportunities, and henceforth act on the principle that moments are grains of gold, by the careful gathering of which you are to become rich in knowledge, in experience, in honor, and in happiness.

I have seen young men starting from the humblest walks and rising to honor, wealth, and influence in the various callings in life. I have seen others, much their superiors in natural talents and external advantages, sink into inefficiency and neglect, unable to acquire any eminence or respect in the world. And when I have inquired for the cause of this difference, I have found almost universally that it was owing to diligence and perseverance in one case, and to negligence and inconstancy in the other. I have rarely known a young man fail to rise in the world who pursued an honest calling with a steady, unwavering purpose to excel in it; and I have never known one fail to sink who was of a slothful, unstable character. Industry and perseverance, coupled with fidelity, can do anything, but without them nothing can be done. Like the tortoise in the fable, it is the slow, sure, perservering runner that first reaches the goal. It is not a few bold, fitful efforts that makes a man of mark. Even the great Newton modestly confessed that he owed his success as a philosopher more to patience and attention than to any original superiority of mind. And we know of many at the present day among the most useful and respected in society, who have risen precisely in the same manner.

Idleness is the nursery of crime. It is that prolific germ of which all rank and poisonous vices are the fruits. It is the source of temptation. It is the field where "the enemy sows tares while men sleep." Could we trace the history of a large class of vices, we should find that they generally originate from the want of some useful employment, and are brought in to supply its place.

XXX.

SELF-CULTURE.

THE secret of moral self-culture lies in training the will to decide according to the fiat of an enlightened conscience. When a question of good or ill is brought before the mind for its action, its several faculties are appealed to. The intellect perceives, compares, and reflects on the suggestions. The emotions, desires and passions, are addressed, and solicited to indulgence. The conscience pronounces its verdict of right or wrong on the proposed act. Then comes the self-determining will, coinciding either with the conscience or the emotions. The end of right moral culture is to habituate it to decide against the passions, desires and emotions, *whenever they oppose the conscience.*

Self-culture may be divided into three classes: the physical, the intellectual, and the moral. In so brief an outline as the few pages before us, we may not be permitted to treat each of these divisions exhaustively. Neither must be developed exclusively. Cultivate the physical unduly and alone, and you may have an athletic savage; the moral, and you have an enthusiast or a maniac; the intellectual, and you have a diseased monstrosity. The three must be wisely trained together to have the complete man.

In our introduction we have already said a few words respecting moral self-culture. As for bodily training, we shall leave that to the gymnasium, shop and plow-handle. Finally, what we have to say to the reader will be mainly under the head of *mental* self-culture. Not necessarily that this branch is of so much more importance than the others, but that knowledge respecting it is least accessible to the general public.

We use the terms Floriculture and Horticulture; why not say *Homoculture?* Is it that the tender floweret and the growing shrub need more care and tending to arrive at maturity and fulfill the object of their creation?

These inanimate flora may grow and mature without culture, but how much would they gladden the earth? What would mankind be in a universal untutored state? He may not be so helpless, nor need so much culture and attention on the part of a higher fostering power, but to be useful to himself or others he must be cultured, or, what is better, *trained*. A man may become expert and ready of wit by *self mental training*.

Herein differs he from the vegetable and brute creation. Let him see to it that he abuses it not. Chatterton says, "God sent his creatures into the world with arms long enough to reach any thing if they choose to be at the trouble."

It is astonishing how much may be accomplished in self-training by the energetic and persevering, who are careful to use fragments of spare time which the idle permit to run to waste.

Excellence is seldom if ever granted to man save as the reward of severe labor.

Thus, Stone learned mathematics while working as a journeyman gardener; thus, Drew studied the highest philosophy in the interval of cobbling shoes ; thus, Miller taught himself geology while working as a day laborer in a quarry.

Whatever one undertakes to learn, he should not permit himself to leave it till he can reach round and clasp hands on the other side.

Dr. Johnson was accustomed to attribute his success to confidence in his own power. Whence came this confidence? He had *tested* his power of reasoning, of loving, of remembering, of application.

One must believe in himself if he would have others believe in him. To think meanly of one's self is to sink in his own estimation.

Cultivate self-help, for in proportion to your self-respect will you be armed against the temptation of low self-indulgence.

Again, "Reverence yourself," as Pythagoras has said. Borne up by this high idea, a man will not defile his body by sensuality, nor his mind by servile thoughts. This thought carried into daily life will be found at the root of all virtues :—cleanliness, sobriety, charity, morality, and religion.

The untutored savage will barter the most

precious diamond and gold for some valueless gew-gaw that may strike his crude fancy. God has garnered our minds with priceless qualities of far more value than precious stones or lustered ore imprisoned in the bosom of the earth.

Shall we catalogue these noble faculties and immediately set about learning their necessity and use? Do not wait for an earthquake or some mighty convulsion to upheave this preciousness, but *dig* it out; so will you be sure of it and prize what you obtain.

To go about whining and bemoaning our pitiful lot, because we fail to achieve success in life—which, after all, depends rather upon habits of industry and attention to business details than upon our knowledge—is the work of a small and often of a sour mind.

Knowledge is power; so is fanaticism, wealth, and a thousand other things. But in your getting, get *wisdom*. It is the trained mind that commands the highest market everywhere. The evidence of this training is expertness in using. The mind of the child before it becomes contaminated and misdirected by the false and often vicious customs of society is on the right and royal road to learning.

In his artlessness he wants to get at the root of every matter bounded by his horizon. Imitate his why, when, and how!

In all correct reasoning and thinking there must be, as with the navigator making out his course at sea, a basis or point from which to begin. If this first point is not rightly located, where would his vessel with its precious freight land? The idea of this self-training is to make us more useful; that we may employ our time and opportunities to greater advantage.

We have to learn how to distinguish between the true and the false. We need not believe a thing because everybody says so. Trace back every thing as far as may be, and find out its truth for yourself. There is no better employment for the mind, nor none that makes it more elastic and ready to render the necessary service when called upon.

The time has arrived when the young man must cast his first vote. It may be a momentous period to him.

How is he to decide correctly? The merits of parties and candidates must be weighed. The process by which he does this is taught in Rhetoric and Logic. It is not necessary that he study these arts by the book to practice the principles laid down in them. In making up a correct judgment respecting any matter, we have first to consider its origin, and then collect and compare the evidence on both sides. Whatever study makes us not better men and citizens is at best an ingenious sort of idleness. Richter said, "I have made as much out of myself as could be made of the stuff, and no man should require more." Self-discipline and self-control are the beginnings of practical wisdom; and these must have root in self-respect. The humblest may say, "To respect myself, to develop myself, this is my duty in life."

Set a high price on your leisure moments. They are sands of precious gold. Properly expended, they will procure for you a stock of great thoughts,—thoughts that will fill, stir, invigorate, and expand your soul.

In rightly improving this time, every one who is earnestly seeking to unfold the native energies of his mind by giving it the food which God designed that it should receive, will soon discover, that, after a night's repose, his mind is clearer and more vigorous than after a day spent in labor, and, perhaps, anxiety; and he will naturally seek to give as much time for study in the morning as possible. Early rising will bring to him a two-fold benefit; it will strengthen both mind and body.

Self-education is something very different from mere reading by way of amusement. It requires prolonged and laborious study. The cultivation of a taste for reading is all very well; but mere reading does little toward advancing any one in the world—little toward preparing him for a higher station than the one he fills. The knowledge which fits a man for eminence in any profession or calling, is not acquired without patient, long-continued, and earnest application.

Mere reading, therefore, although of importance in itself, as a means of enlarging our ideas and correcting and refining our tastes, does not give a man much power—does not help him to rise above the position in which circumstances may have originally placed him. It is *study* that does this. Franklin the printer's boy did not become Franklin the philosopher and statesman, by reading only, but by study; and we do not hear of his studying under teachers, and of being guided by them—for, like many of us, he did not possess these high advantages,—but his education progressed under the supervision of his own mind. He had to feel his way along, and to correct his own errors, ever and anon, as the dawning of fresh light enabled him to see them. And you may do the same; you, with few acquirements now, and few opportunities, may, if you only will it, become as useful and eminent a man as Franklin. But you must work for it. Diligently and earnestly must you labor, or you cannot stand side by side, in after years, with the men who have become distinguished for the important services they have been able to render their fellows.

Any one to become great through his own exertions has undertaken a large contract. But the perspective of this superstructure looks larger and more formidable than it is in reality.

One is likely to look at a successful life, rounded out and complete, and then measure his own life by this model. He must not say, "I cannot do as these men do, but rather I should try to do what they have done."

These models, whose memories are finger-posts for a succeeding generation, did not become such by accident nor by a single leap. No! they rose by successive single degrees, each of which was wrought out by sweating brow and aching muscle.

The late Vice-President, Henry Wilson, in speaking of his early life, said: "I was born in poverty. Want sat on my cradle. I know what it is to ask a mother for bread when she has none to give."

He was nurtured in adversity, had a vigorous constitution, and, above all, had an inspiration. He read with avidity whatever books came in his way.

The first month after he was twenty-one years of age, he spent in driving team, cutting mill-logs, etc., working at the rate of fifteen hours a day and receiving for it the magnificent sum of six dollars! Speaking of this event, he says, "Those dollars looked as large to me as the moon looks to-night."

The after events of his history are written upon the hearts of his countrymen. He never received dollars, place, nor renown, that was not the distinct reward and outcome of his own honest exertions. Therefore his life ought to furnish an incentive, and be an encouragement for every boy and young man.

Abraham Lincoln, our first martyred President, in his early life of privation and toil and his successive victories, presents another grand example, worthy the imitation of all. His noble integrity and honesty became proverbial. So pure was he in his life and so worthy of trusts, great and small, that he was needed to fill such positions. He needed not to seek them, they sought him. It was not commanding ability, nor great genius, that made him sought after; constituencies and business firms knew their interests were safe and exalted in his keeping. Young reader, you need no better title to fame and excellence.

There is yet another of whom we would speak; one whose name was heard and reverenced in every home, and whose image was enshrined within every heart. His life, beginning in the humblest manner, was filled full with grandeur and greatness. Who of modern history have their names enrolled so high for scholastic attainments, and broad intellectual training; and the only chance outside of his own energy and perseverance was in having a noble and judicious mother. Other mothers may have been honored by their sons, but none ever received a more reverential kiss, than the mother of James A. Garfield, on the day of the inauguration of her noble son as the Chief Magistrate of fifty millions of willing and loyal subjects.

We have presented to the reader the names and brief sketches of the lives of several men, as striking illustrations of self training. Their histories are in every library, and almost in every household. Their early years were filled with trials, struggles such as but few readers of these pages have any realizing sense.

Study these lives; the secret of their success is not shrouded in mystery.

Look for good examples, imitate them.

You are, or soon will be, a man, and called upon to take an active part in life's affairs. You will either lead or be led.

Think whether you will be a voter all your life or be voted for. Think whether you will please those who bid, or bid those you please.

Whose brains will you use? Do you intend to work all day for just what will last you over night?

When you see a man fail, be sure there is a reason. Search it out. Remember friends are made. Relations grow.

There are ages yet to live. It may not be on this earth but somewhere. The grave is the lock which must be opened before we can touch or enjoy the treasures beyond its dark keeping—before we can go to the punishments or rewards that await us.

The golden crop cannot be garnered till after the seed has been sown. The impression cannot be read till after the type is set in order, and the errors shown in the proof. Stones do not, of themselves, turn up as you pass by to reveal the golden wealth hidden beneath them.

Labor will win. The rose does not spring from chaos to the bosom of the bride.

Let us look around us, and see the rich earth, the laughing brook, which lover-like kisses the lips of its guide, and runs joyously on.

See the deep woods—listen to the birds as they sing—look on the flowery sentinels of beauty—follow the deep shadows till they rest on your own heart—look up—*up*—UP, beyond the leafy roof, and into the deep blue of heaven. Stand on the sea-shore—observe the millions of shells, once homes for wondrous life—listen to what the wild waves are saying—hear the sea-spirit sullenly moaning down the shore, and then THINK.

But usually young men are not willing to devote themselves to that process of slow, toilsome self-culture, which is the price of great success. Could they soar to eminence on the lazy wings of genius, the world would be filled with great men. But this can never be; for, whatever aptitude for particular pursuits Nature may donate to her favorite children, she conducts none but the laborious and the studious to distinction.

The great thoughts of great men are now to be procured at prices almost nominal. Therefore, you can easily collect a library of choice authors. Public lectures are also abundant in our large cities. Attend the best of them, and carefully treasure up their richest ideas. But, above all, learn to reflect even more than you read. Reading is to the mind what eating is to the body; and reflection is similar to digestion. To eat, without giving nature time to assimilate the food to herself by the slower process of digestion, is to deprive her, first, of health, and then, of life; so, to cram the intellect by reading, without due reflection, is to weaken and paralyze the mind. He who reads thus has "his perceptions dazzled and confused by the multitude of images presented to them."

There are a very large number of young men, just entering upon life, of good minds, but deficient education, who from this cause, are kept back, and labor under great disabilities. Many of these are mechanics, and others have no regular calling whatever, and find it very difficult to earn anything beyond a very meagre support. Upon these we would urge, with great earnestness, the duty of self-education, so called. The deficiencies of early years need not keep them back from positions of eminence in society—those positions awarded only to men of intellectual force and sound information—if they will but strive for them. A vast amount of knowledge may be gained in the course of a very few years, by rightly employing those leisure hours which every one has; and this knowledge, if of a practical kind, will always insure to a man the means of elevation in the world.

XXXI.

CHARACTER.

THERE is a difference between character and reputation. Character is what we really are. Reputation is what others suppose we are. A man may have a good character and a bad reputation, or he may have a good reputation and a bad character. The reason of this is, that we form our opinions of men from what they appear to be, and not from what they really are. Some men appear to be much better than they really are, while others are better than they appear to be. Most men are more anxious about their reputation than they are about their character. This is improper. While every man should endeavor to maintain a good reputation, he should especially labor to possess a good character. Our true happiness depends not so much on what is thought of us by others, as on what we really are in ourselves. Men of good character are generally men of good reputation; but this is not always the case, as the motives and actions of the best men are sometimes misunderstood and misrepresented. But it is important, above everything else, that we be right, and do right, whether our motives and actions are properly understood and appreciated or not. Nothing can be so important to any man as the formation and possession of a good character.

The influences which operate in the formation of character are numerous, and however trivial some of them may appear, they are not to be despised. The most powerful forces in nature are those which operate silently and imperceptibly. This is equally true of those moral forces which exert the greatest influences on our minds, and give complexion to our character. Among these, early impressions, example, and habits, are perhaps the most powerful.

Early impressions, although they may appear to be but slight, are the most enduring, and exert the greatest influences on the life. By repetition they acquire strength, become deeply rooted in the mind, and give bent and inclination to its powers. "The tiniest bits of opinion sown in the minds of children in private life, afterwards issue forth to the world, and become its public opinion; for nations are gathered out of nurseries." Examples, it is said, preach to eyes; and there are but few persons, especially among the young, who can avoid imitating those with whom they associate. For the most part, this is so unconscious that its effects are almost unheeded, but its influence is not on that account the less permanent. The models which are daily placed before us, tend to mould our character and shape our course in life. Habit results from the repetition of the same act, until we become so accustomed to it, that its performance requires no mental effort, and scarcely attracts our attention.

By the influence of early impressions, the force of example, and the power of habit, the character becomes slowly and imperceptibly, but at length decidedly formed; the individual acquires those traits and qualities by which he is distinguished, and which bear directly upon his happiness and welfare. It is very important, then, for every one, and especially for the young, to be very careful as to the impressions he cherishes, the example he imitates, and the habits he forms. These are important elements which go to constitute character, and if they are of an improper nature, the result will be ruinous. Character is everything. It matters not what a man's reputation may be, without a good character he cannot be happy.

In the formation of a good character, it is of great importance that *the early part of life be improved and guarded* with the utmost diligence and carefulness. The most critical period of life is that which elapses from fourteen to twenty-one years of age. More is done during this period, to mould and settle the character of the future man than in all the other years of life. If a young man passes this season with pure morals and a fair reputation, a good name is almost sure to crown his maturer years, and descend with him to the close of his days. On the other hand, if a young man, in this spring season of life, neglects his mind and heart; if he indulges himself in vicious courses, and forms habits of inefficiency and slothfulness, he experiences a loss which no efforts can retrieve, and brings a stain upon his character which no tears can wash away.

"A fair reputation, it should be remembered, is a plant, delicate in its nature, and by no means rapid in its growth. It will not shoot up in a night, like the gourd that shaded the prophet's head ; but like that same gourd, it may perish in a night." A character which it has cost many years to establish, is often destroyed in a single hour, or even minute. Guard, then, with peculiar vigilance, this forming, fixing season of your existence ; and let the precious days and hours that are now passing by you, be diligently occupied in acquiring those habits of intelligence, of virtue and enterprise, which are so essential to the honor and success of future life.

To the formation of a good character, it is of the highest importance that you *have a commanding object in view, and that your aim in life be elevated.* To this cause, perhaps, more than to any other, is to be ascribed the great difference which appears in the characters of men. Some start in life with an object in view, and are determined to attain it; whilst others live without plan, and reach not for the prize set before them. The energies of one are called into vigorous action, and they rise to eminence, whilst the others are left to slumber in ignoble ease, and sink into obscurity.

The happiness of all with whom you are or shall be connected in life, is deeply involved in the characters you are now forming. Those kind parents who watched over your infancy and childhood, and who are looking to you as the props of their declining age; those brothers and sisters, who are allied to you by ties of the tenderest affection; all your dear relatives and friends, regard, with deep and anxious solicitude, the course upon which you are entering, and the habits which are to stamp the character and fix the destiny of your future life. In no way can you contribute so much to the happiness of all who esteem and love you, as by sustaining a good character; and in no way pierce their hearts with keener sorrow, than by compelling them to behold you sacrificing a fair reputation, and all your prospects for life, in unworthy and vicious indulgences.

Another thing demanded of you by society is *an upright and virtuous character*. If a young man is loose in his principles and habits; if he lives without plan and without object, spending his time in idleness and pleasure, there is more hope of a fool than of him. He is sure to become a worthless character, and a pernicious member of society. He forgets his high destination as a rational, immortal being; he degrades himself to a level with the brute; and is not only disqualified for all the serious duties of life, but proves himself a nuisance and a curse to all with whom he is connected.

No young man can hope to rise in society, or act worthily his part in life, without a fair moral character. The basis of such a character is virtuous principle; or a deep, fixed sense of moral obligation, sustained and invigorated by the fear and love of God. The man who possesses such a character can be trusted. Integrity, truth, benevolence, justice, are not with him words without meaning; he knows and he feels their sacred import, and aims, in the whole tenor of his life, to exemplify the virtues they express. Such a man has decision of character;—he knows what is right, and is firm in doing it. Such a man has independence of character;—he thinks and acts for himself, and is not to be made a tool of to serve the purposes of party. Such a man has consistency of character;—he pursues a straightforward course, and what he is to-day you are sure of finding him to-morrow. Such a man has true worth of character;—and his life is a blessing to himself, to his family, to society, and to the world.

We contend that no man can rationally hope to pass the ordeals of life in safety, unless his outward virtues derive vitality and vigor from an inward religious life. To be perennial, the stream must proceed from a living spring; to be fruitful, the tree must spread its roots in a congenial soil; so, to insure the possession of uprightness through the manifold trials of human life, the soul of a man must be in harmony with its Creator,— through faith in Him, it must derive strength to resist wrong, to desire and to will right, when standing in the plunging torrent of evil influences which is ever dashing down the highways of trade. Greatly good men are always "like solitary towers in the city of God; and secret passages, running deep beneath external nature, give their thoughts intercourse with higher intelligences, which strengthens and controls them."

Recollect your high destination, as rational and immortal beings, and remember, that your all, both for this and the future world, depends on the manner in which you form your character. If, during the few years in which your characters are forming, you shun the paths of vice, and carefully cultivate habits of virtue, intelligence, and good conduct, you cannot fail to rise to respectability, and usefulness, and happiness. You will have the sweet approbation of your own minds to cheer and animate you; friends will rise up to patronize and encourage you, Providence will smile upon your efforts and ways; and your life, crowned with the blessings of God and the gratitude of your fellow men, will decline in peace, and give a fair promise of a bright rising in another world.

XXXII.

VICE.

> Vice is a monster of so frightful mien,
> As to be hated needs but to be seen;
> Yet seen too oft, familiar with her face,
> We first endure, then pity, then embrace.—POPE.

MEN, for the most part, are but little aware of the danger which attends the *beginnings of evil*. They readily perceive the degrading and destructive tendency of the grosser vices; but they are slow of heart to believe that there are certain dispositions and habits which inevitably lead to those vices and their consequent degradation and ruin. While they are careful to shun the more open and flagrant offences, they are not afraid to venture upon what are deemed little sins,—upon slight deviations from duty,—occasional indulgence of the appetites and passions.

No young man becomes suddenly abandoned and profligate. There is always a gradual progress. He begins in *slight, occasional departures* from rectitude, and goes on from one degree of guilt to another, till conscience becomes seared, the vicious propensity strong, the habit of indulgence fixed, and the character ruined.

Take for example, a young man, who occasionally drinks to excess in the social circle; he does not dream that he is entering upon a course which will probably end in confirmed intemperance. He means no harm; he says of sin, is it not a little one; there can be no danger in this. But soon his bands are made strong, and he becomes the slave of a sottish vice.

One of the greatest artifices the devil uses to engage men in vice and debauchery, is to attach names of contempt to certain virtues; and to fill weak souls with a foolish fear of passing for scrupulous, should they desire to put them in practice. Sometimes those boast of abstinence who have lost their digestive power; those boast of chastity whose blood is cold and stagnant; those boast of knowing how to be silent who have nothing to say. In short, mankind make vices of the pleasures which they cannot enjoy, and virtues of the infirmities to which they are subject. We sometimes clap vice in fetters and then call it virtue. Some men are kind because they are dull, as common horses are easily broken to harness. Some are orderly because they are timid, like cattle driven by a boy with a wand. And some are social because they are greedy, like barn-yard fowls that mind each other's clucking. Many persons think themselves perfectly virtuous because, being well fed, they have no temptation to vice. They don't distinguish between virtue and victuals.

Vice is like the terrible cobra di capello which winds itself round its victim, and from its deadly fangs pours poison into his blood. So vice enslaves and destroys. Whoever is charmed to its embraces, finds himself enfolded in bonds of might, and poisoned with a morbid venom which irritates and stimulates his passions beyond the endurance of his vital powers; until, with a diseased body, a hardened heart, and a remorseful spirit, he sinks to an untimely death, and is driven to stand, shivering with fear, before his God!

On the other hand, the man who seriously considers the nature and design of his being; who shuns the society and flees from the amusements of the thoughtless and the vicious; who devotes his vacant hours to the improvement of his mind and heart, and aims at the acquisition of those habits and virtues which may qualify him for the duties of life,—cannot fail to rise in respectability, in influence and honor.

His virtues and attainments make room for him in society, and draw around him the confidence and respect, the affection and support, of all worthy and good men.

Never open a door to a little vice, lest a great one should enter also. Small faults indulged are little thieves that let in greater. Many a man's vices have at first been nothing worse than good qualities run wild. Vice, abstractly considered, is often engendered in idleness, but, the moment it becomes efficiently vice, it must quit its cradle and cease to be idle. Vice lives and thrives by concealment. Why does no man confess his vices? It is because he is yet in them. It is for a *waking* man to tell his dreams. Human frailty is no excuse for criminal immorality. We may hate men's vices without any ill-will to their persons; but we cannot help despising those that have no kind of virtue to recommend them.

The plea of every young mind that enters upon its novitiate in the school of vice is for only a little self-indulgence. The mind, while undefiled by positive contact with the sins of the senses, revolts from the idea of a wholly vicious life. It views such a life as the dogs of Egypt are said to fear the crocodiles which abound in the Nile. So intense is this fear, that, when impelled by fierce thirst to drink its waters, they do it as they run, not daring to pause long enough at once to satisfy their burning desires. Thus does the young man propose to taste illicit joys. He would only *taste* and flee, lest he should be devoured! Alas! he knows not the terrible power he awakens, when he quaffs his first draught from the prohibited stream of pleasure! By that one act, he casts away the talisman of his safety, self-denial; he removes the curb from the mouth of lust, he pours foul water upon the virgin snow, and thus places an ineffaceable stain upon his purity, he contracts guilt, sows the seed of remorse, and sells his moral freedom for naught. A little indulgence? Never, young man! Allow it, and you are lost; blindness begins where vice first enchants. Beware, oh beware of this pestilential apology! Be like the knights of Tasso, who, on Armida's enchanted isle, seeing all the enticements of sense voluptuously prepared and inviting to indulgence, exclaimed:

> "Let us avoid the dream
> Of warm desire, and in resolve be strong;
> Now shut our ears to the fair Siren's song,
> And to each smile of feminine deceit
> Close the fond eye."

XXXIII.

POVERTY.

A MAN should not be despised because he is poor. Even to slight the poor is mean. To be poor is more honorable than to be dishonorably rich. Pious poverty is better than poor piety. Poverty breeds wealth; and wealth, in its turn, breeds poverty. The earth, to form the mound, is taken out of the ditch; and the height of one is near about the depth of the other. Wealth and poverty are both temptations: that, tends to excite pride; this, discontent. The privations of poverty render us too cold and callous, and the privileges of property too cold and consequential; the first place us beneath the influence of opinion — the second above it. Poverty induces and cherishes dependence, and dependence strengthens and increases corruption. Whoever is not contented in poverty, would not be perfectly happy with riches. Bulwer says that poverty is only an idea in nine cases out of ten. Some men with ten thousand dollars a year suffer more for want of means than others with three hundred. The reason is, the richer man has artificial wants. His income is ten thousand, and, by habit, he spends twelve or fifteen thousand, and he suffers enough from being dunned for unpaid debts to kill a sensitive man. A man who earns a dollar a day, and does not run in debt, is the happier of the two. Very few people who have never been rich will believe this; but it is as true as God's word. There are people, of course, who are wealthy and enjoy their wealth, but there are thousands upon thousands with princely incomes who never know a moment's peace, because they live above their means. There is really more happiness in the world among the working people than among those who are called rich. It is contrary to God's law of nature for a man to live in idleness. He who lives by the "sweat of his brow," is the happiest. In large cities many people are unhappy for want of employment. If their lot had been cast in the country, where they tilled the sea for their own account, this would never happen. Poverty has, in large cities, very different appearances. It is often concealed in splendor, and often in extravagance. It is the care of a very great part of mankind to conceal their indigence from the rest. They support themselves by temporary expedients, and every day is lost in contriving for to-morrow. Have the courage to appear poor, and you disarm poverty of its sharpest sting. Let it be said, that though he is poor, yet he always pays his debts. He that has much and wants more is poor; he who has little and wants no more is rich.

"Poor and content, is rich, and rich enough."—SHAK.

The poor man's purse may be empty, but he has as much gold in the sunset and as much silver in the moon as anybody. The richer a man is the more he dreads poverty; thus poverty looks most frightful at a distance. Want is little to be dreaded, when a man has but a short time left to be miserable. Of all poverty, that of the mind is most deplorable. None but God and the poor know what the poor do for each other. Nature is a great believer in compensations. Those to whom she sends wealth, she saddles with lawsuits and dyspepsia. The poor never indulge in woodcock, but they have a style of appetite that converts a mackerel into a salmon, and that is quite as well. To miss a fortune is not necessarily a misfortune. Blessed may be the stroke of disaster that sets free the children of the rich, giving them over to the hard but kind bosom of poverty. If there is anything in the world, says Dr. Holland, that a young man should be more grateful for than another, it is the poverty which necessitates his starting in life under very great disadvantages. Poverty is one of the best tests of human quality in existence. A triumph over it is like graduating with honor at West Point. It demonstrates stuff and stamina. It is a certificate of worthy labor faithfully performed. A young man who cannot stand this test, is not good for anything. He can never rise above a drudge or a pauper. A young man who cannot feel his will harden if the yoke of poverty presses upon him, and his pluck rise with every difficulty that poverty throws in his way, may as well retire into some corner and hide himself. Poverty saves a thousand times more men than it ruins ; for it only ruins those who are not particularly worth saving, while it saves multitudes of those whom wealth has ruined. I pity you, my rich young friend, because you are in danger. You lack one great stimulus to effort and excellence, which your poor companion possesses. You will be very apt, if you have a soft spot in your head, to think yourself above him, and that sort of thing makes you mean, and injures you. With full pockets and full stomach, and good linen and broadcloth on your back, your heart and soul plethoric, in the race of life you will find yourself surpassed by all the poor boys around you, before you know it. No, my boy ; if you are poor, thank God and take courage, for he intends to give you a chance to make something of yourself. If you had plenty of money, ten chances to one it would spoil you for all useful purposes. Do you lack education? Have you been cut short in the text book? Remember that education, like some other things, does not consist in the multitude of things a man possesses. What can you do? That is the question that settles the business for you. Do you know your business? Do you know men, and how to deal with them? Has your mind, by any means whatsoever, received that discipline which gives to it action, power and facility? If so, then you are more a man, and a thousand times better educated, than the fellow who graduates from a college with his brains full of stuff that he cannot apply to the practical business of life—stuff, the acquisition of which has been in no sense a disciplinary process, so far as he is concerned. There are very few men in this world less than thirty years of age, and unmarried, who can afford to be rich. One of the greatest benefits to be reaped from great financial disasters, is the saving of a large crop of young men.

XXXIV.

ABILITY AND OPPORTUNITY.

WE must wrestle in this world if we do not care to lie down, and form a pavement for other men's cars of triumph.

Is ability inherent or acquired?

Men do differ as to the quantity and qualty of their morals, intellects and physical powers.

Do these degrees of gifts account for the difference of attainments? No! Very few do all that they *can* do. More lies in willingness and determination than in inherent ability.

How frequently is it said: "I could do this or that if I wanted to or had the opportunity."

The world is full of people who think they can do, or have done, great things.

Success in this life is not measured by what might be done, but rather by what is set about and really accomplished.

The success of the great can usually be traced to small and patient beginnings.

Consult earnestly the biographies of the successful ones, and you will find that the secret of their success depended not so much upon their natural abilities, as their willingness and determination to do with their might whatsoever their minds or hands found to do.

Do not wait for Providence to open up a path for you. You are on the earth; you exist. Make the most of that, and thus conform to the great natural law of cause and effect.

It is not so much what we possess in natural acquirements as what we make use of and become expert in.

Life is not only a voyage, but a ladder, the steps of which should not be retraced. The top of this ladder cannot be reached by a single leap, but must be ascended by successive single steps.

You may think unfortuitous chance has placed you in an uncongenial position. No matter, do the best you can, and you will grow and gain by the trying. The eaglet does not soar to the clouds in his first flight. He gets there eventually, whether his first lessons are practiced from the plain or mountain craig. Therefore fly, strive, climb in whatever position you may be placed.

In every human being there are great possibilities. It is not all of life to live or be. Our existence is made up of component parts, and he who knows most of life all the way through can be of most service to, and in the world.

How does opportunity or chance, as it would be termed by some, enter into life's calculation; what part does it play in the voyage of life?

What do we mean by such frequent use of this magic word—chance? Is it that when the Divine One created us, He ordained that at this or that episode in our experience, certain material advantages would be put in our way, by which, if we would but embrace them, fortune, reputation and happiness would be ours?

Those who have acquired wisdom would

tell us to put aside such notions of fatalism, and depend upon our own natural shrewdness and foresight.

What God's will respecting us is, we may not know specifically. But we may be sure that it best pleases Him for us to make the most and noblest use of our life in detail. We must not wait for the handwriting on the wall, nor for the voice from the cloud.

The history of France would have been very differently written if Napoleon had remained in Egypt, waiting for the Directory to call him home. He knew he was the man for the situation. But that knowledge alone did not satisfy him. He waited not for the opportunity or chance, but he made or created it; simply acting according to his best judgment. The "Star of Austerlitz" had not yet arisen.

Most, if not all of us, know what we ought, and what would be best for us to do, but we lack the inclination.

Do not wait for something to turn up, nor for that "Tide in the affairs of men which taken at its flood leads on to fortune."

If God so arranged these ebbs and flows of fortune's tides, He also so managed that man should know the times and seasons thereof, in order to take advantage of the same.

Let us rather conclude that there are openings, chances, or opportunities, all along this path of life, not waiting for us indeed, but with us every day.

It might be a very desirable thing for humanity were there human genius exalted enough to say to this one, "go here," and to that one, "go there,"—"this or that place you are divinely appointed to fill."

As it is, too many float along this voyage, waiting indifferently or wearily, saying to themselves: "Kismet,—God wills it."

All have ability enough; and accompanying nature's gifts, are the necessary opportunities. Let us embrace a few of these opportunities at a time, cultivate earnestly the fundamentals, the primary best elements of our natures. This is sowing the seed in the spring time.

The tiny seed takes root and forces its shoots up through and out of its prison into the air and sunlight above, where all may behold it fulfilling its destiny. But it had to be sown before it could expand and grow. This growing was done quietly, and the breaking through the soil was the inevitable result of the sowing.

This condition of things does not inaptly represent certain phases of our own life. Action or exertion in any fruitful direction is the result of some impulse. This action may produce some little complete result, but does it stop there? By no means; other results, unconsciously on the actor's part, perhaps, must grow out of this. Nor does the good result stop even here, but each thing well done creates the next opportunity. Labor, therefore, at the first thing that comes to hand; perform that duty well, and so with each day's duties. Other and more congenial and profitable occupation will of necessity grow out of these duties well performed. Lives so filled out need not to wait for many chances.

Some young men of early promise, whose hopes, purposes, and resolves were as radiant as the colors of the rainbow, fail to distinguish themselves, because they are not willing to devote themselves to that toilsome culture which is the price of great success. Whatever aptitude for particular pursuits Nature may donate to her favorite children, she conducts none but the laborious and the studious to distinction.

Reader, behold faintly outlined, the picture of two lives. One does nothing but simply wait for the thing that he thinks he is fitted for to turn up—the other has been in constant training, making or creating opportunities that he fills as fast as his own indomitable energy brings them to the surface.

These are the conditions of success. Give a man power and a field in which to use it, and he must accomplish something. He may not do and become all that he desires and dreams of, but his life cannot be a failure. I never hear men complaining of the want of ability. The most unsuccessful think that they could do great things if they only had a chance. Somehow or other something or somebody has always been in the way. Providence has hedged them in so that they could not carry out their plans. They knew just how to get rich, but they lacked opportunity.

Sit down by one who thus complains and ask him to tell you the story of his life. Before he gets half through he will give you occasion to ask him, "Why didn't you do so at that time? Why didn't you stick to that piece of land and improve it, or to that business and develop it? Is not the present owner of that property rich? Is not the man who took up the business you abandoned successful?" He will probably reply: "Yes, that was an opportunity; but I did not think so then. I saw it when it was too late." In telling his story he will probably say, of his own accord, half a dozen times, "If I had known how things were going to turn I might have done as well as Mr. A. That farm of his was offered to me. I knew that it was a good one, and cheap, but I knew that it would require a great deal of hard work to get it cleared and fenced, to plant trees, vines, etc., and to secure water for irrigation. I did not like to undertake it. I am sorry now that I didn't. It was one of my opportunities."

The truth is, God gives to all of us ability and opportunities enough to enable us to be moderately successful. If we fail, in ninety-five cases out of a hundred it is our own fault. We neglect to improve the talents with which our Creator endowed us, or we failed to enter the door that he opened for us. A man cannot expect that his whole life shall be made up of opportunities, that they will meet him at regular intervals as he goes on, like milestones by the roadside. Usually he has one or two, and if he neglects them he is like a man who takes the wrong road where several meet. The further he goes the worse he fares.

A man's opportunity usually has some relation to his ability. It is an opening for a man of his talents and means. It is an opening for him to use what he has, faithfully and to the utmost. It requires toil, self-denial and faith. If he says, "I want a better opportunity than that. I am worthy of a higher position than it offers;" or if he says, "I won't work as hard and economize as closely as that opportunity demands," he may, in after years, see the folly of his pride and indolence.

There are young men all over the land who want to get rich, and yet they scorn such opportunities as A. T. Stewart and Commodore Vanderbilt improved. They want to begin, not as those men did, at the bottom of the ladder, but half way up. They want somebody to give them a lift, or carry them up in a balloon, so that they can avoid the early and arduous struggles of the majority of those who have been successful. No wonder that such men fail, and then complain of Providence. Grumbling is usually a miserable expedient that people resort to to drown the reproaches of conscience. They know that they have been foolish, but they try to persuade themselves that they have been unfortunate.

XXXV.

BEAUTY.

BEAUTY has been called "the power and aims of woman." Diogenes called it "woman's most forcible letter of recommendation." While a modern author defines it "a bait that as often catches the fisher as the fish." Nearly all the old philosophers denounced and ridiculed beauty as evanescent, worthless and mischievous; but, alas! while they preached against it they were none the less its slaves. None of them were able to withstand "the sly, smooth witchcraft of a fair young face." A really beautiful woman is a natural queen in the universe of love, where all hearts pay a glad tribute to her reign.

Nature, in many other works, has scattered her beauty with an unsparing hand; but none of them impress so strongly upon the mind the *idea* of beauty as the female countenance. The flower may be more delicate in its formation, and may show a more exquisite color —the wide-spread meadow may display its beauty, and fields, and groves, and winding streams may variegate the scene; yet all that is here presented fades before the female countenance. In the countenance of man, there is a certain majesty of look, which is not found in the other sex; yet where is that softness, that sweet heavenly smile that plays upon the countenance of a female—where is that splendor that dazzles the eye of the beholder—that expression that baffles all description. The more we compare the female countenance with any other object, the more shall we be inclined to give the former the palm of loveliness, and the more ready to exclaim with nature's sweet poet:

> "Where is any author in the world,
> Teaches such beauty as a woman's eye?"

As among females there are some which are superior to others, so there are also some seasons when the female countenance excels in loveliness. I have seen her shine in all the vivacity and splendor of the assembly, partaking in the common gayety and enjoying the pleasures of the scene, with all the liveliness of youthful spirits. I have seen her at the fireside, attending to the management of domestic concerns—while her presence seemed to banish care, and her converse enlightened the family circle. I have seen her reposing in gentle sleep, when her eye was unconscious of my look — when the gentleness of her slumbers told that innocence was seated in her breast; but never yet did I see female so lovely as when affliction had rent her bosom, and had chased the smile from her cheek. Affliction, however, though it had deprived her countenance of its vivacity, had given a softening expression to her features, which added to her loveliness. Her eyes were uplifted, in calm resignation, as if imploring help from Him, who is the father of the fatherless, and the comforter of the afflicted.

The most fascinating women are those that can most enrich the every day moments of existence. In particular and attaching sense, they are all those that can partake our pleasures and our pains in the liveliest and most devoted manner. Beauty is little without this. Beauty without virtue, is a flower without perfume. Virtue is the paint that can smooth the wrinkles of age.

The violet will soon cease to smile. Flowers must fade. The love that has nothing but beauty to sustain it soon withers away. A pretty woman pleases the eye; a good woman, the heart. The one is a jewel, the other a treasure. Invincible fidelity, good humor, and complacency of temper, outlive all the charms of a fine face, and make the decay of it invisible.

Beauty has been not unaptly, though perhaps rather vulgarly, defined as "all in the eye," since it addresses itself solely to that organ, and is intrinsically of little value. From this ephemeral flower spring many of the ingredients of matrimonial unhappiness. It is a dangerous gift for both its possessor and its admirer. If its possession, as is often the case, turns the head, while its loss sours the temper, if the long regret of its decay outweighs the fleeting pleasure of its bloom, the plain should pity rather than envy the handsome. Beauty of countenance, which, being the light of the soul shining through the face, is independent of features or complexion, is the most attractive as well as the most enduring charm. Nothing but talent and amiability can bestow it, no statue or picture can rival it, and time itself cannot destroy it. Beauty, dear reader, is the woman you love the best—whatever she may seem to others.

The secret of beauty is contentment. To be at peace with ourselves and our condition and surroundings is more to be prized than wealth or position. And this treasure lies within the power of each. Its possession depends entirely upon ourselves, and it should be deep and abiding. A cheerful, happy face, the mirror of a serene and peaceful mind, can give more real pleasure to your family than money. It can spread sunshine in the abode of poverty. Solomon well says that a contented mind is a continual feast. Contentment is opposed to fretting and crossness and frowns; and these never help matters. Chronic ill-humor sets its seal upon the face in lines never to be erased, and we instinctively avoid such people. Good-humor and serenity also make their mark. and attract us by their loveliness.

Personal beauty is a letter of recommendation written by the hand of divinity, but frequently dishonored by the bearer. An enemy of beauty is a foe to nature. We are always less prone to admit the perfection of those for whom our approbation is demanded; and many a woman has appeared comparatively plain in our eyes, from having heard her charms extolled, whose beauty might otherwise have been readily admitted. As a want of exterior generally increases the interior beauty, we should perhaps generally do well to judge of woman as the impressions on medals — pronouncing those the most valuable which are the *plainest*. Nature seldom lavishes many of her gifts upon one subject : the peacock has no voice ; the beautiful Camellia Japonica has no odor ; and belles frequently have no great share of intellect. Beauties sometimes die old maids. They set such a value on themselves that they don't find a purchaser until the market is closed. She who studies her glass, neglects her heart. A beautiful woman if poor should use a double circumspection; for her beauty will tempt *others*, her poverty *herself*. "Thine was a dangerous gift," says the poet Rogers, "the gift of beauty; would thou hadst less, or wert as once thou wast." Many and varied are the female charms that conquer us. Here we find a woman whose strength, like Samson's, is in her hair; a second holds your affections by her teeth; and a third is a Cinderella, who wins hearts by her pretty little foot. But she is the most beautiful woman whom we love most; and the woman we love the most is frequently the one to whom we talk of it the least.

An author says, there are two sorts of persons which are not to be comforted; a rich man who finds himself dying, and a beauty when she finds her charms fading. As flowers fade, and the waters flow to the ocean, so youth and beauty pass away, and our years hasten to eternity.

XXXVI.

LOVE.

WOMAN loves more than man because she sacrifices more. For every woman it is with the food of the heart as with that of the body ; it is possible to exist on a very small quantity, but that small quantity is an absolute necessity. Woman loves or abhors ; man admires or despises. Woman without love is a fruit without flavor. In love, the virtuous woman says *no ;* the passionate says *yes ;* the capricious says *yes* and *no ;* the coquette neither *yes* nor *no.* A coquette is a rose from whom every lover plucks a leaf; the thorn remains for the future husband. She may be compared to tinder which catches sparks, but does not always succeed in lighting a *match.* Love, while it frequently corrupts pure hearts, often purifies corrupt hearts. How well he knew the human heart who said, " we wish to constitute all the happiness, or if that cannot be, the misery of the one we love." Reason is only the last resource of love.

He that loves upon the account of virtue, can never be weary ; because there are always fresh charms to attract and entertain him. Solid love, whose root is virtue, can no more die than virtue itself. It is by no means certain that Mark Anthony, when he gave the world for love, didn't make a sharp bargain.

He who loves a lady's complexion, form and features, loves not her true self, but her soul's old clothes. The love that has nothing but beauty to sustain it, soon withers and dies. The love that is fed with presents always requires feeding.

Some writer asserts that "a French woman will love her husband if he is either witty or chivalrous ; a German woman, if he is constant and faithful ; a Dutch woman, if he does not disturb her ease and comfort too much ; a Spanish woman, if he wreaks vengeance on those who incur his displeasure ; an Italian woman, if he is dreamy and poetical ; a Danish woman, if he thinks that her native country is the brightest and happiest on earth; a Russian woman, if he despises all Westerners as miserable barbarians; an English woman, if he succeeds in ingratiating himself with the court and the aristocracy; an American woman, if—he has plenty of money."

There are two classes of disappointed lovers —those who are disappointed before marriage, and the more unhappy ones who are disappointed after it. To be deprived of a person we love is a happiness in comparison of living with one we hate.

At first it surprises one that love should be made the principal staple of all the best kinds of fiction; and perhaps it is to be regretted that it is only one kind of love that is chiefly depicted in works of fiction. But that love itself is the most remarkable thing in human life, there cannot be the slightest doubt. For, see what it will conquer. It is not only that it prevails over selfishness, but it has the victory over weariness, tiresomeness and familiarity. When you are with the person loved, you have no sense of being bored. This humble and trival circumstance is the great test—the only sure and abiding test of love. With the persons you do not love you are never supremely at your ease. You have some of the sensation of walking upon stilts. In conversation with them, however much you admire them and are interested in them, the horrid idea will cross your mind of "What shall I say next?" Converse with them is not perfect association. But with those you love, the satisfaction in their presence is not unlike that of the relations of the heavenly bodies to one another, which, in their silent revolutions, lose none of their attractive power. The sun does not talk to the world, but it attracts it.

The love which survives the tomb, is one of the noblest attributes of the soul. If we still love those we lose, we cannot altogether lose those we love. Oh, man, fear not for thy affections, and feel no dread lest time should efface them! There is neither to-day nor yesterday in the powerful echoes of memory —there is only always. He who no longer feels, has never felt. There are two memories —the memory of the senses, which wears out with the senses, and in which perishable things decay; and the memory of the soul, for which time does not exist, and which lives over, at the same instant, every moment of its past and present existence. Fear not, ye who love. Time has power over hours, none over the soul. Love is the great instrument and engine of nature, the bond and cement of society, the spring and spirit of the universe. It is of that active, restless nature, that it must of necessity exert itself; and like the fire, to which it is so often compared, it is not a free agent to choose whether it will heat or no, but it streams forth by natural results, and unavoidable emanations, so that it will fasten upon an inferior, unsuitable object, rather than none at all. The soul may sooner leave off to subsist than to love, and like the vine, it withers and dies if it has nothing to embrace.

That love is the leading element of the highest happiness in marriage; that love, while it lasts, covers a multitude of errors, privations, misfortunes—even sins—I do not doubt. But the question is, how far is love, when unaccompanied by any other of the conditions which I have mentioned as belonging to a perfect marriage, itself a justification of marriage? True love works wonders; but it cannot prevent the physical and mental ailments which develop themselves in people of feeble organisms. It cannot supply a lack of intelligence, a want of force in either husband or wife; and, as all housekeepers know, it cannot "make the pot boil." Love alone, when we consider its proverbial instability, and the small chance it has of surviving under bleak conditions, is certainly an insufficient capital upon which to commence the partnership of marriage. This is true of even the highest and strongest loved; how much more so of the hasty and passionate attachments which lead to so many thousands of marriages! There is an infinity of false sentiment about the passion of love. While I would not cast a doubt upon the existence of noble love, of devotion, and of passion which no sorrow or trial can tire, which is even refined and strengthened by suffering, yet the value, the office, the very nature of love in our ordinary life is greatly misunderstood. Love is the most exaggerated passion in literature. It holds in our imagination a position which it does not hold in the life of one man or woman in a thousand. "Being the supreme passion of modern art," says a recent writer, "it becomes necessary to sound high its praises. We should suppose, if we read only novels and poetry, that the one thing interesting in life is the relation of the sexes and the anxieties of pairing. Many young people are so dizzy with love that they are unable to go on with the other interests of life. They cannot see men as they are, engaged in their daily work, pursuing their various ends and living a multifarious life, of which love is but a single element." Our regard for the passion oversteps the healthy limit, and becomes morbid; we judge of it untruly; we attend to its promptings with absurd expectations, we teach ourselves that the passion is uncontrollable, and regard it as a kind of fate; and we glorify the supremacy of a first love, as if the heart did not require a training as varied as the intellect. Considering the widespread misery which our misconceptions of love have wrought, we might doubt whether this passion was not the greatest misfortune as well as the greatest blessing in the world. We may conclude, in spite of Chaucer, that love's allegiance is not the *only* thing needful to make a permanently happy marriage.

XXXVII.

COURTSHIP.

THE ostensible object of courtship is the choice of a companion. For no other object should any intercourse having the appearance of courtship be permitted or indulged in. It is a species of high handed fraud upon an unsuspecting heart, worthy of the heaviest penalty of public opinion, or law. The affections are too tender and sacred to be trifled with. He who does it is a wretch. He should be ranked among thieves, robbers, villains, and murderers. He who steals money steals trash; but he who steals affections without a return of similar affections, steals that which is dearer than life and more precious than wealth. His theft is a robbery of the heart.

How little is thought of the first buddings of love between two young persons! By the parents it is often deemed a fitting subject for

joke and laughter. The parties themselves, conscious chiefly of a mutual attraction, abandon themselves to romantic visions of future bliss, and to efforts to please each other. Little do they dream that from their gay and lightsome intercourse is to proceed a stream of exquisite delight, or of burning poison, running parallel, perhaps, with their immortal existence. Yet so it is. A life of bitter, bitter anguish, or of as much happiness as is permitted to mortals on earth, lies enclosed in the, but too lightly esteemed, state of courtship. Next to marriage, it is the gravest and most solemn affair relating to life this side the grave.

One of the meanest things a young man can do, and it is not at all of uncommon occurrence, is to monopolize the time and attention of a young girl for a year, or more, without any definite object, and to the exclusion of other gentlemen, who, supposing him to have matrimonial intentions, absent themselves from her society. This selfish "dog-in-the-manger" way of proceeding should be discountenanced and forbidden by all parents and guardians. It prevents the reception of eligible offers of marriage, and fastens upon the young lady, when the acquaintance is finally dissolved, the unenviable and *unmerited* appellation of "flirt." Let all your dealings with women, young man, be frank, honest, and noble. That many whose education and position in life would warrant our looking for better things, are culpably criminal on these points, is no excuse for *your* short-comings. That woman is often injured, or wronged, through her holiest feelings, adds but a blacker dye to your meanness. *Treat every woman you meet as you would wish another man to treat your innocent, confiding sister.*

Courtships are the sweet and dreamy thresholds of unseen Edens, where half the world has paused in couples, talked in whispers, under the moonlight, and passed on, and never returned. Little squalls don't upset the lover's boat; they drive it all the faster to port.

Courtship, says the Rev. G. S. Weaver, should not seek to captivate, but to learn real character. Love character, not person merely. Feeling, not reason, leads astray. Courting the wrong way is by impulse, and not judgment; by a process of wooing, and not of discovery; an effort to please, and not a search for companionship; with excitement, and not with calmness and deliberation; in haste, and not with cautious prudence; a vision of the heart, and not a solemn reality; conducted by feeling, and not by reason; so managed as to be a perpetual blandishment of pleasure the most intoxicating and delightful, and not a trying ordeal for the enduring realities of solid and stubborn life; a perpetual yielding up of everything, and not a firm maintenance of everything that belongs to the man or woman. In almost every particular false, and hence must be followed by evil consequences.

The young man and young woman who form a solemn matrimonial alliance at any age before they have attained manhood and womanhood, do it more in folly than in wisdom, more in passion than in love, do it at the risk of their life's peace, and the most fearful consequences that follow in the train of such matrimonial adventures. It can only be called a matrimonial adventure. They do it in childish ignorance. It is not possible for a youth at that age to have a judgment sufficiently matured, and a heart sufficiently subdued, to render him capable of forming an absolutely correct opinion upon a subject of such vast importance and such complicated results. Treat it lightly as you will, it is a subject of the most momentous importance to human virtue, prosperity and happiness, and involves much of the most intricate and profound philosophy of human life, conduct and character. A subject of such importance requires the matured powers of manhood and womanhood, and the experience and observation of such maturity.

Many young ladies indulge in very nonsensical opinions, or, rather notions, concerning love. They foolishly fancy themselves bound to be "smitten," to "fall in love," to be "love-sick," with almost every silly idler who wears a fashionable coat, is tolerably good-looking, and pays them particular attention. Reason, judgment, deliberation, according to their fancies, have nothing to do with love. Hence, they yield to their feelings, and give their company to young men, regardless of warning advice or entreaty. A father's sadness, a mother's tears, are treated with contempt, and often with bitter retorts. Their lovers use flattering words, and, like silly moths fluttering round the fatal lamp, they allow themselves to be charmed into certain misery. Affection is founded upon esteem; estimable qualities in a man can alone secure the continuance of connubial love; if these are not in him, love has no foundation, it is unreal, and will fall, a wilted flower, as soon as the excitement of youthful passion is overpast.

Passion leads us into a dream-land of folly. Time dissolves the airy fabric of the fancy, and the soul awakes to mourn, disconsolate, amid the ruins which surround it. Listen not, therefore, to the voices of passion. Heed your reason. Keep the precious love of your young heart, until you find a partner every way worthy of it. You have no treasure like that love. Bestow it unworthily, and you are hopelessly ruined. Give it to some pure heart, full of noble qualities, and you will drink joy from a pure fountain.

With every young lady the paramount question concerning him who offers her particular attentions, ought to be, "Is he worthy of my love?" Her first aim should be to decide it. She should observe him well and thoughtfully, —study his character as it may be expressed in his counteannce, his words, spirit, and actions. Through her parents she should inquire into his previous history, and learn especially IF HE HAS BEEN A DUTIFUL SON AND AN AFFECTIONATE BROTHER. This last is a vital test, though it is generally overlooked; but it is very sure, that a young man devoid of filial and fraternal love, will not, can not make a good husband.

In the free, social intercourse of a young lady with her friends of the other sex, the idea of love, or a particular preference of one over the other, should never be permitted to enter her mind. She should look upon them as her intelligent friends, and feel that their association was for mutual advantage in elevating the mind, improving the taste, and strengthening the moral principles.

There is a popular feeling that it is somewhat a disgrace for a woman to pass through life unmarried; and shrinking from that obloquy, multitudes marry according to the forms of law when they are not drawn together by any qualities of mind and soul, and there is no true marriage of heart. What wonder, then, that discontent and misery arise, and a divorce, if not sought, is often desired! Those who regard love as a flame that comes as a flash of gunpowder, must not feel disappointed if the blackness and desolation that succeed a gunpowder flash is all that is left after their brief infatuation is over. All love before marriage should be a study for love after marriage. If not well understood, its power is apt to become exhausted. The power of love must be measured not by its intensity, but by its effects; by its beneficence in bringing into play a higher range of motives, by the facilities it unfolds, by its skill in harmonizing different natures.

Nine out of ten look upon marriage as a gambling fair—to snatch an article at a venture; and consider the prizes are not much more numerous in the one than in the other. When there are fewer secret manœuvres and tricks of courtship before marriage, there will be less unhappiness after. How often we see couples who are "engaged" trying to hide little foibles and eccentricities from the one they are expecting to live a life-time with! How blind such a course is! Then, if ever, the true characteristics of each should appear! If anything is objectionable before marriage, how much more so after, when a lie is added to it! Live true lives when you are "courting." Better an engagement should be broken off, than a life should be wasted. Many counsel the young not to expect too much of love. That is an evil philosophy, however, which advises to moderation by undervaluing the possibilities of a true and glorious love. Happiness in this life depends more upon the capacity of loving than on any other single quality. If men lose all the treasure of love, it does not prove that the treasure is not to be found, but that they have not sought aright. Many men dig for diamonds in love, and only find pebbles in wedded life. The diamonds are there, however, only they know not how to dig for them.

XXXVIII.

MARRIAGE.

THIS is a subject upon which very few *think* seriously, and those who make it a matter of much reflection too generally think erroneously.

The great difficulty, with regard to those who most need proper instruction on this subject, is, that they will not hearken to what is said to them, but either follow the leadings of impulse and passion, or look with cool deliberation to the attainment of some selfish end. In either case, mutual unhappiness is the almost inevitable result.

Whoever marries without having just ideas of so important a relation, runs great danger of committing an error that will render turbid for life all the well-springs of happiness.

When the honeymoon passes away, setting behind dull mountains, or dipping silently into the stormy sea of life, the trying hour of married life has come. Between the parties there are no more illusions. The feverish desire for possession has gone, and all excitement receded. Then begins, or should, the business of adaptation. If they find that they do not love one another as they thought they did, they should double their assiduous attentions to one another, and be jealous of everything which tends in the slightest way to separate them. Life is too precious to be thrown away in secret regrets or open differences. And let me say to every one to whom the romance of life has fled, and who are discontented in the slightest degree with their conditions and relations, begin this reconciliation at once. Renew the attentions of earlier days. Draw your hearts close together. Talk the thing all over. Acknowledge your faults to one another, and determine that henceforth you will be all in all to each other; and my word for it, you shall find in your relation the sweetest joy earth has for you. There is no other way for you to do. If you are happy at home, you must be happy abroad; the man or woman who has settled down upon the conviction that he or she is attached for life to an uncongenial yoke-fellow, and that there is no way of escape, has lost life; there is no effort too costly to make which can restore to its setting upon the bosom the missing pearl.

If it be scarcely possible for two persons connected by the ties of common friendship, to live constantly together, or even habitually to pass much time in mutual society, without gradually approaching nearer and nearer in their sentiments and habits; still less probable is it, that from the closest and most attractive of all bands of union a similar effect should not be the result. The effect will be experienced by both parties, and perhaps in an equal degree. But if it be felt by one in a greater degree than by the other, it seems likely to be thus felt by the husband. In female manners inspired by affection, and bearing at once the stamp of modesty and of good sense, example operates with a captivating force which few can resist.

But, whatever be the influence which the amiable virtues of a wife may obtain over her husband; let not the consciousness of it ever lead her to seek opportunities of displaying it, nor to cherish a wish to intrude into those departments which belong not to her jurisdiction. Content with the province which reason and revelation have assigned to her, and sedulous to fulfil, with cheerful alacrity, the duties which they prescribe; let her equally guard against desiring to possess undue weight over her husband's conduct, and against exercising amiss that which properly belongs to her.

Married people should never be without a home of their own, from the day when they are united to the day of their death. By giving it up, they may save money and avoid trouble, but they are sure to lose happiness and substantial comfort, and a great part of the best uses of life. This is true at all times: but there are no five years in which it is so important as those in which it is most frequently disregarded.

Home life is the proper and normal condition of marriage, and they who have no home of their own are not much better than half married, after all.

The objection made is the expense. They

cannot afford the first outlay, and the continued expenditure involved. To which we might give a first and general answer, that until we can afford to provide a home we have no business to be married. But we admit that the objection lies deeper and is more difficult of removal than at first appears. It consists in foolish habits of expenditure and in absurd social ambition, by which unreal necessities are created, and the problem of domestic life is made one of almost impossible solution. It is this which either prevents marriage or destroys its comfort. When a young woman who is accustomed to live and dress like a princess, and a man who has always expended his whole income on himself, contract an alliance, they must either have a large income to maintain the accustomed style, or adopt the very unaristocratic expedient of "lodgings," so as to keep up the appearance before the world, and economize in comfort for the sake of being extravagant in show. How much there is of this let every American city declare. A part of the evil, and no small part, is the fault of parents, who train their daughters so that nothing but wealth can make them happy, and economy is a virtue vulgar and hateful in their eyes; but chiefly it is a general lack of good sense, false ideas of respectabilty, the want of independence, and almost servile subjection to the opinion of what we call the world, which generally means some fifteen or twenty of the silliest persons of our acquaintance.

Two things are essential to the happiness of married life: First, to have a home of one's own; and, second, to establish it upon such a scale as to live distinctly and clearly within one's means—if possible, not quite up to them, and *by no possibility* beyond them. A great proportion of the failures in wedlock may be traced directly to the neglect of the latter rule. No man can feel happy or enjoy the comfort of his own fireside, who is spending more than he earns. Debt destroys his self-respect, puts him at variance with the world, and makes him irritable, ill-tempered, and hard to please. There is no Christian virtue, no Christian grace, that can keep company with the burdensome annoyance of debt. The thought of unpaid bills, and of rent falling due and unprovided for, destroys the relish of one's food and awakens him from the soundest sleep at night, and the luxuries for which the debts were contracted become loathsome in his sight. Then comes fault-finding and recrimination, and love flies out at the window when the sheriff threatens to come in at the door. Romantic people may talk as much as they please about indulgent husbands and fascinating wives, but the plain matter of fact is, that no attraction or charms in the wife, either of person or of mind, are more available in keeping the husband's affection and respect, than the despised virtues of economy and thrift. By such care for his interests she confers daily benefits upon him, she lessens and cheers his labor, she increases his credit, and enlarges his prosperity; "She will do him good and not evil all the days of her life."

We are not so absurd as to sing the praise of poverty, for no one remains poor when he can help it; but it certainly has its compensations, and they who are afraid of marriages, or being married, deny themselves the luxury and inherent respectability of a home, because their house must be small and their furniture poplar instead of rose-wood, do not deserve to be happy. Let them begin according to their means, however small, and honestly living within them be contented with what they have. Every added comfort, as they go onward, will be prized, and if wealth be at last attained it will be enjoyed, while those who begin at the top of earthly prosperity can at the best only remain there, and in the mutations of human affairs are most likely to come down. The truth is that, as already said, happiness, in any respectable sense of the word, depends very little upon what we have, and almost entirely upon what we are.

The husband and wife who literally take care of each other, depending comparatively little upon the vexatious intervention of servants, at the same time enjoy the duty and appreciate the kindness. The comforts which one owes directly to the wife's diligent and affectionate care and industry, are wonderfully different from those which money buys and are brought by mercenary hands. The costly gifts of riches, involving no labor or inconvenience, are prized for their splendor and beauty, and are accepted, perhaps as tokens of regard; but they are not half so precious as gifts, comparatively trifling, made valuable by the consecration of pains-taking and self-denial. I speak to many who have tried both experiences—who began in the most humble and moderate manner and have gradually worked upward—and they would all testify that, after the positive inconvenience of straitened circumstances had passed, the happiest part of life was in the enjoyment of neither riches nor poverty, of moderate circumstances and quiet domestic life. They look back to those days as the happiest, when by mutual helping they gave and received the proofs of affection and tenderness.

Marriage is to a woman, at once the happiest and saddest event of her life ; it is the promise of future bliss, raised on the death of all present enjoyment. She quits her home, her parents, her companions, her occupations, her amusements—her everything upon which she has hitherto depended for comfort—for affection, for kindness, for pleasure. The parents by whose advice she has been guided, the sister to whom she has dared impart every embryo thought and feeling, the brother who has played with her, in turns the counselor and the counseled, and the younger children to whom she has hitherto been the mother and the playmate—all are to be forsaken in one instant; every former tie is loosened, the spring of every hope and action to be changed, and yet she flies with joy into the untrodden paths before her. Buoyed up by the confidence of requited love, she bids a fond and grateful adieu to the life that is past, and turns with excited hopes and joyous anticipations of the happiness to come.

Leigh Hunt concludes an essay on marriage as follows: " There is no one thing more lovely in this life, more full of the divinest courage, than when a young maiden, from her past life, from her happy childhood, when she rambled over every field and moor around her home; when a mother anticipated her wants and soothed her little cares; when brothers and sisters grew from merry playmates to loving, trustful friends; from the Christmas gatherings and romps, the summer festivals in bower or garden; from the rooms sanctified by the death of relatives; from the holy and secure backgrounds of her childhood, and girlhood, and maidenhood, looks out into a dark and unillumined future, away from all that, and yet unterrified, undaunted, leans her fair cheek upon her lover's breast, and whispers, 'Dear heart! I cannot see, but I believe. The past was beautiful, but the future I can trust *with thee!*'"

Then woe to the man who can blast such hopes—who can, coward-like, break the illusions that have won her, and destroy the confidence which his love inspired.

XXXIX.

AFTER MARRIAGE.

MANY a woman has gone into her room and had a "good cry" because her husband called her by her baptismal name, and not by some absurd nickname invented in the days of their folly; or because, pressed for time, he hurried out of the house without going through the established formula of leave-taking. The lover has merged into the husband; security has taken the place of wooing; and the woman does not take kindly to the transformation. Sometimes she plays a dangerous game, and tries what flirting with other men will do. If her scheme does not answer, and her husband is not made jealous, she is revolted, and holds herself that hardly-used being, a neglected wife. She cannot accept as a compliment the quiet trust which certain cool-headed men of a loyal kind, place in their wives; and his tolerance of her flirting manner—which he takes to be manner only, with no evil in it, and with which, though he may not especially like, he does not interfere—seems to her indifference rather than tolerance. Yet the confidence implied in this forbearance is, in point of fact, a compliment worth all the *petits soins* ever invented, though this hearty faith is just the thing which annoys her, and which she stigmatizes as neglect. If she were to go far enough she would find out her mistake. But by that time she would have gone too far to profit by her experience.

Nothing is more annoying than that display of affection which some husbands and wives show to each other in society. That familiarity of touch, those half-concealed caresses, those absurd names, that prodigality of endearing epithets, that devoted attention which they flaunt in the face of the public as a kind of challenge to the world at large, to come and admire their happiness, is always noticed and laughed at. Yet to some women this parade of love is the very essence of married happiness, and part of their dearest privileges.

They believe themselves admired and envied, when they are ridiculed and scoffed at; and they think their husbands are models for other men to copy, when they are taken as examples for all to avoid. Men who have any real manliness, however, do not give in to this kind of thing; though there are some as effeminate and gushing as women themselves, who like this sloppy effusiveness of love, and carry it on into quite old age, fondling the ancient grandmother with gray hairs as lavishly as they had fondled the youthful bride, and seeing no want of harmony in calling a withered old dame of sixty and upwards by the pet names by which they had called her when she was a slip of a girl of eighteen. The continuance of love from youth to old age is very lovely, very cheering; but even "John Anderson, my Jo," would lose its pathos if Mrs. Anderson had ignored the difference between the raven locks and the snowy brow. This public display of familiar affection is never seen among men who pride themselves on making good lovers, as certain men do—those who have reduced the practice of love-making to an art, a science, and know their lesson to a letter.

These men are delightful to women, who like nothing so much as being made love to, as well after marriage as before ; but men who take matters quietly, and rely on the good sense of their wives to take matters quietly, too, sail round these scientific adorers for both depth and manliness. And if women knew their best interests they would care more for the trust than the science.

All that excess of flattering and petting of which women are so fond, becomes a bore to a man if required as part of the daily habit of life. Out in the world as he is, harassed by anxieties of which she knows nothing, home is emphatically his place of rest, where his wife is his friend who knows his mind, where he may be himself without fear of offending, and relax the strain that must be kept up out of doors ; where he may feel himself safe, understood, and at ease. And some women, and these by no means the coldest or the least loving, are wise enough to understand this need of rest in the man's harder life, and accepting the quiet of security as part of the conditions of marriage, content themselves with the undemonstrative love into which the fever of passion has subsided. Others fret over it, and make themselves and their husbands wretched because they cannot believe in that which is not forever paraded before their eyes. Yet what kind of a home is it for the man if he has to walk as if on egg-shells, every moment afraid of wounding the susceptibilities of a woman who will take nothing on trust, and who has to be continually assured that he still loves her, before she will believe that to-day is as yesterday? Of one thing she may be certain; no wife who understands what is the best kind of marriage demands these continual attentions, which, voluntary offerings of the lover, become enforced tribute from the husband. She knows that as a wife, whom it is not necessary to court or flatter, she has a nobler place than that which is expressed by the attentions paid to a mistress. Wifehood, like all assured conditions, does not need to be buttressed up, but a less certain position must be supported from the outside, and an insecure self-respect, an uncertain holding, must be perpetually strengthened and reassured. Women who cannot live happily without being made love to are more like mistresses than wives, and come but badly off in the great struggles of life and the cruel handling of time. Placing all their happiness in things which cannot continue, they let slip that which lies in their hands, and in their desire to retain the romantic position of lovers, lose the sweet security of wives. Perhaps, if they had higher aims in life than those with which they make shift to satisfy themselves, they would not let themselves sink to the level of this folly, and would understand better than they do now the worth of realities as contrasted with appearances. And yet we cannot but pity the poor, weak, craving souls who long so pitifully for the freshness of the morning to continue far into the day and evening, who cling so tenaciously to the fleeting romances of youth. They are taken by the glitter of things—love-making among the rest; and the man who is the showiest in his affection, who can express it with the most color, and paint it, so to speak, with the minutest touches, is the man whose love seems to them the most trustworthy and the most intense. They often make the mistake of confounding this show with the substance, of trusting to pictorial expression rather than solid facts. And they often make the mistake of cloying their husbands with personal half-childish caresses, which were all very well in the early days, but which become tiresome as time goes on and the gravity of life deepens. And then, when the man quietly keeps them off, or more brusquely repels them, they are hurt and miserable, and think the whole happiness of their lives is dead, and all that makes marriage beautiful at an end. What is to be done to balance things evenly in this unequal world of sex? What, indeed, is to be done at any time to reconcile strength with weakness, and to give each its due? One thing at least is sure. The more thoroughly women learn the true nature of men, the fewer mistakes they will make, and the less unhappiness they will create for themselves; and the more patient men are with the hysterical excitability, the restless craving, which nature, for some purpose at present unknown, has made the special temperament of women, the fewer *femmes incomprises* there will be in married homes, and the larger the chance of married happiness.

The great secret is, to learn to bear with each other's failings; not to be blind to them —that is either an impossibility or a folly; we must see and feel them; if we do neither, they are not evils to us, and there is obviously no need of forbearance; but, to throw the mantle of affection around them, concealing them from each other's eyes; to determine not to let them chill the affections; to resolve to cultivate good-tempered forbearance, because it is the only way of mitigating the present evil, always with a view to ultimate amendment. Surely, it is not the perfection, but the imperfection, of human character that makes the strongest claim in love. All the world must approve, even enemies must admire the good and the estimable in human nature. If husband and wife estimate only that in each which all must be constrained to value, what do they more than others? It is infirmities of character, imperfections of nature, that call for pitying sympathy, the tender compassion, that makes each the comforter, the monitor of the other. Forbearance helps each to attain command over themselves. Few are the creatures so utterly evil as to abuse a generous confidence, a calm forbearance. Married persons should be preeminently friends, and fidelity is the great privilege of friendship. The forbearance here contended for is not a weak and wicked indulgence of each other's faults, but such a calm, tender observation of them as excludes all harshness and anger, and takes the best and gentlest methods of pointing them out in the full confidence of affection.

The very nearest approach to domestic felicity on earth is in the mutual cultivation of an absolute unselfishness. Never talk at one another either alone or in company; never both manifest anger at once; never speak loud to one another, unless the house is on fire; never reflect on a past action, which was done with a good motive and the best judgment at the time; let each one strive to yield oftenest to the wishes of the other; let self-abnegation be the daily aim and effort of each; never find fault, unless it is perfectly certain that a fault has been committed, and always speak lovingly; never taunt with a past mistake; neglect the whole world besides rather than one another; never allow a request to be repeated; never make a remark at the expense of the other, it is a meanness; never part for a day without loving words to think of during absence; never meet without a loving welcome; never let the sun go down on any anger or grievance; never consider any fault you have committed settled until you have frankly confessed it and asked forgiveness; never forget the happy hours of early love; never sigh over what might have been, but try to make the best of what is; never forget that marriage is ordained of God, and that His blessing alone can make it what it should ever be; never be contented till you know you are both walking in the narrow way; never let your hopes rest upon anything this side of the eternal home. Preserve the privacies of your house, your marriage state and your hearts from father, mother, sister, brother and all the world. Between you two let no third person come to share the secret joy or grief that belongs to yourselves alone. Do you two, with God's help, build your own quiet world, not allowing your dearest earthly friend to be the confidant of aught that concerns your domestic peace.

Let moments of alienation, if they occur, be veiled and forgotten in moments and years of faithful, devoted love, but never let the wall of another's confidence be built up between you and your wife's or your husband's heart. Promise this to yourselves and to each other. Renew the vow at every temptation; you will find your account in it; your souls will grow, as it were, together, and at last be as one. Ah, if many a young pair had on their wedding day known this all-important secret, how many marriages would have been happier than, alas, they are!

Be not weary in well-doing. An old story contains a lesson which many married couples have not yet learned. When Jonathan Trumbull was Governor of Connecticut, a gentleman called at his house one day requesting a private interview. He said: "I have called upon a very unpleasant errand, sir, and want your advice. My wife and I do not live happily together, and I am thinking of getting a divorce. What do you advise, sir?" The governor sat a few moments in thought; then turning to his visitor, said, "How did you treat Mrs. W—— when you were courting her? and how did you feel toward her at the time of your marriage?" Squire W—— replied, "I treated her as kindly as I could, for I loved her dearly at that time." "Well, sir," said the governor, "go home and court her now just as you did then, and love her as when you married her. Do this in the fear of God for one year, and then tell me the result." When a year passed away Squire W—— called again to see the governor, and said: "I have called to thank you for the good advice you gave me, and to tell you that my wife and I are as happy as when first we were married. I cannot be grateful enough for your good counsel." "I am glad to hear it, Mr. W——," said the governor, "and I hope you will continue to court your wife as long as you live."

Addison has left on record the following important sentence: "Two persons who have chosen each other out of all the species, with the design to be each other's mutual comfort, and entertainment, have in that very action bound themselves to be good humored, affable, joyful, forgiving and patient, with respect to each other's frailties and imperfections, to the end of their lives." Mr. Henry says: "I have heard of a married couple who, though they were both of a hasty temper, yet lived comfortably together by simply observing a rule on which they had mutually agreed, viz.: 'Never to be both angry at the same time;'" and he adds, that an ingenious and pious father was in the habit of giving this advice to his children, when they were married:

"Doth one speak fire? t'other with water come!
Is one provok'd? be t'other soft and dumb."

The following good counsel is from a wife and mother: "I will try to make myself and all around me agreeable. It will not do to leave a man to himself till he comes to you, to take no pains to attract him, to appear before him with a long face. It is not so difficult as you think, dear child, to behave to a husband so that he shall remain forever a husband. I am an old woman, but you can still do as you like; a word from you at the right time will not fail of its effect; what need have you to play the part of suffering virtue? The tear of a loving girl, says an old book, is like a dewdrop on a rose; but that on the cheek of a wife is a drop of poison to her husband. Try to appear cheerful and contented, and your husband will be so; and when you have made him happy, you will become so in reality. Nothing flatters a man so much as the happiness of his wife; he is always proud of himself as being the source of it. As soon as you are cheerful you will be lively and alert, and allow no opportunity for speaking an agreeable word to pass. Your education, which gives you an immense advantage, will greatly assist you, and your sensibility will become the noblest gift that nature has bestowed on you, when it shows itself in affectionate assiduity, and stamps on every action a soft, kind, tender character, instead of wasting itself in secret repinings."

Let both parties consider, when they enter upon the duties of domestic life, that the rights of each are equal; and let each feel that it is as much a duty to *do right* as to *exact right*. Let each consider, that, being brought up in different families, and under different influences, it is but natural to expect that each should have opinions, and perhaps prejudices, different from the other; and that the right of each to his, or her, opinion, is equal to that of the other. Let each remember, that the happiness of life depends upon harmony,— that nothing will be gained by strife. Hence, let each consider whether his, or her peculiar notions, are matters of principle, or matters of opinion and taste. If the former, let each regard the other's as sacred. Do not trifle with them. If the latter, let each one consider the liability of every one to err, and try to think and feel alike. Talk over the matter, not for the purpose of convincing, but for the purpose of understanding each other. Weigh each other's reasons fairly, and be willing to give all reasonable credit. In a matter of principle, it will also be proper, if both agree, for each to state the subject of difference fairly, and give the reasons for the difference. Reflect much upon the points of difference with a view to the reconciliation of differences, and always be ready to yield a point when convinced of error. On all important subjects, as they affect the interests of both, take counsel together before acting. Whatever affects both should be understood and decided by both. Avoid having separate interests. Whatever may be said in favor of these, they are certainly unnatural in domestic life, and cannot fail to mar domestic happiness. There can be no separate interests—whatever affects one must affect the other. Never deceive each other. The loss of confidence is one of the greatest evils that can befall a married pair. It destroys all domestic comfort, and renders home a scene of turmoil and confusion. When confidence is lost, all is lost. In fine, let each strive to please the other, even in little things ; (the whole of life is made up of little things ;) and you will not fail to please. If you see a fault in your companion, think if you have not greater, and be as ready to correct your own, as to require a correction of your companion. Let each lay aside every cause of offense to the other, that everything may go on smoothly, that the burden of life may be easily borne.

XL.

ADVANTAGES OF WEDLOCK.

"When a man hath taken a new wife he shall not go to war, neither shall he be charged with any business; but he shall be free at home one year, and cheer up the wife which he has taken."—Deut. 24:5.

A MAN who avoids matrimony on account of the cares of wedded life, cuts himself off from a great blessing for fear of a trifling annoyance. He rivals the wiseacre who secured himself against corns by having his legs amputated. In his selfish anxiety to live unencumbered, he only subjects himself to a heavier burden; for the passions, that apportion to every individual the load he is to bear through life, generally say to the calculating bachelor—" As you are a single man you shall carry double." The *Assurance Magazine*, an English periodical, makes the statement, that in the two periods of life, 20 to 25 and 25 to 30, the probability of a widower marrying in a year is nearly three times as great as that of a bachelor; at 30 it is four times as great; at 60 the chances of a widower marrying in the year is eleven times as great as that of a bachelor. After the age of 30 the probability of a bachelor marrying in a year diminishes in a most rapid ratio; the probability at 35 is not much more than half that at 30, and nearly the same proportion exists between each period of five years afterwards. None but the married man has a home in his old age. None has friends then, but he; none but he knows and feels the solace of the domestic hearth; none but he lives and freshens in his green old age, amid the affections of his children. There is no tear shed for the old bachelor; there is no ready hand and kind heart to cheer him in his loneliness and bereavement; there is none in whose eyes he can see himself reflected, and from whose lips he can receive the unfailing assurances of care and love. He may be courted for his money; he may eat and drink and revel; and he may sicken and die in a hotel or a garret, with plenty of attendants about him, like so many cormorants waiting for their prey ; but he will never know the comforts of the domestic fireside.

The guardians of the Holborn Union lately advertised for candidates to fill the situation of engineer at the workhouse, a single man, a wife not being allowed to reside on the premises. Twenty-one candidates presented themselves, but it was found that as to testimonials, character, workmanship, and appearance, the best men were all married men. The guardians had therefore to elect a married man.

A married man, falling into misfortune, is more apt to retrieve his situation in the world than a single one, chiefly because his spirits are soothed and retrieved by domestic endearments, and his self-respect kept alive by finding, that although all abroad be darkness and humiliation, yet there is a little world of love at home over which he is a monarch. Jeremy Taylor says, " If you are for pleasure, marry ; if you prize rosy health, marry. A good wife is heaven's last best gift to man—his angel of mercy—minister of graces innumerable—his gem of many virtues—his casket of jewels— her voice, his sweetest music—her smiles, his brightest day—her kiss the guardian of innocence—her arms the pale of his safety, the balm of his health, the balsam of his life—her industry, his surest wealth—her economy, his safest steward—her lips, his faithful counsellors—her bosom the softest pillow of his cares—and her prayers the ablest advocates of heaven." He considered marriage " a nursery of heaven," and " the greatest interest in the world next to the last throw for eternity."

Doubtless you have remarked with satisfaction, says a writer in *Frazer's Magazine*, the little oddities of men who marry rather late in life are pruned away speedily after marriage. You may have found a man who used to be shabbily and carelessly dressed, with huge shirt-collar frayed at the edges, and a glaring yellow silk pocket-handkerchief, broken of these and become a pattern of neatness. You have seen a man whose hair and whiskers were ridiculously cut, speedily become like other human beings. You have seen a clergyman who wore a long beard in a little while appear without one. You have seen a man who used to sing ridiculous sentimental songs leave them off. You have seen a man who took snuff copiously, and who generally had his breast covered with snuff, abandon the vile habit. A wife is the grand wielder of the moral pruning knife. If Johnson's wife had lived, there would have been no hoarding of bits of orange peel; no touching all the posts in walking along the street; no eating and drinking with a disgusting voracity. If Oliver Goldsmith had been married, he would never have worn that memorable and ridiculous coat. Whenever you find a man whom you know little about, oddly dressed, or talking ridiculously, or exhibiting any eccentricity of manner, you may be tolerably sure that he is not a married man. For the little corners are rounded off, the shoots are pruned away, in married men. Wives generally have much more sense than their husbands, especially when the husbands are clever men. The wife's advices are like the ballast that keeps the ship steady. They are like the wholesome though painful shears snipping off the little growths of self-conceit and folly.

Robert Southey says a man may be cheerful and contented in celibacy, but I do not think he can ever be happy; it is an unnatural state, and the best feelings of his nature are never called into action. The risks of marriage are for the greater part on the woman's side. Women have so little the power of choice, that it is not perhaps fair to say that they are less likely to choose well than we are; but I am persuaded that they are more frequently deceived in the attachments they form, and their opinions concerning men are less accurate than men's opinion of their sex. Now, if a lady were to reproach me for having said this, I should only reply that it was another mode of saying there are more good wives in the world than there are good husbands, which I verily believe. I know of nothing which a good and sensible man is so certain to find, if he looks for it, as a good wife.

Somebody has said, "before thou marry, be sure of a house wherein to tarry." And see, my friend, that you make your house a *home*. A house is a mere skeleton of bricks, laths, plaster, and wood; a home is a residence not merely of the body but of the heart. It is a place for the affections to develop themselves—for children to love, and learn, and play in—for husband and wife to toil smilingly together to make life a blessing. A house where a wife is a slattern and a sloven cannot be a home; a house where there is no happy fireside, no book, no newspaper—above all, where there is no religion and no Bible, how can it be a home? My bachelor brother, there cannot, by any possibility, be a home where there is no wife. To talk of a home without love, we might as well expect to find a New England fireside in one of the pyramids of Egypt.

There is a world of wisdom in the following: "Every schoolboy knows that a kite would not fly unless it had a string tying it down. It is just so in life. The man who is tied down by half-a-dozen blooming responsibilities and their mother, will make a higher and stronger flight than the bachelor who, having nothing to keep him steady, is always floundering in the mud. If you want to ascend in the world, *tie* yourself to somebody."

> "Jenny is poor, and I am poor,
> Yet we will wed—so say no more;
> And should the bairnies to us come,
> As few that wed but do have some;
> No doubt but heaven will stand our friend,
> And bread as well as children send;

ADVANTAGES OF WEDLOCK.

So fares the hen in the farmer's yard,
To live alone she finds it hard;
I've known her weary every claw,
In search of corn among the straw;
But when in quest of nicer food,
She clucks among her chirping brood;
With joy we see the self-same hen,
That scratched for one co'd scratch for ten.
These are the tho'ts that make me willing
To take my girl without a shilling;
And for the self-same cause, you see,
Jenny resolves to marry me."

XLI.

TELL YOUR WIFE.

IF you are in any trouble or quandary, tell your wife—that is if you have one—all about it at once. Ten to one her invention will solve your difficulty sooner than all your logic. The wit of woman has been praised, but her instincts are quicker and keener than her reason. Counsel with your wife, or mother or sister, and be assured, light will flash upon your darkness. Women are too commonly adjudged as verdant in all but purely womanish affairs. No philosophical students of the sex thus judge them. Their intuitions, or insights, are the most subtle. In counseling a man to tell his wife, we would go farther, and advise him to keep none of his affairs a secret from her. Many a home has been happily saved, and many a fortune retrieved, by a man's full confidence in his "better half." Woman is far more a seer and

prophet than man, if she be given a fair chance.

We will say nothing of the manner in which that sex usually conduct an argument; but the *intuitive judgments of women* are often more to be relied upon than the conclusions which we reach by an elaborate process of reasoning. No man that has an intelligent wife, or who is accustomed to the society of educated women, will dispute this. Times without number you must have known them decide questions on the instant, and with unerring accuracy, which you had been poring over for hours, perhaps, with no other result than to find yourself getting deeper and deeper into the tangled maze of doubts and difficulties. It were hardly generous to allege that they achieve these feats less by reasoning than by a sort of sagacity which approximates to the sure instinct of the animal races; and yet there seems to be some ground for the remark of a witty French writer, that, when a man has toiled step by step up a flight of stairs he will be sure to find a woman at the top; but she will not be able to *tell how she got there*. How she got there, however, is of little moment. If the conclusions a woman has reached are sound, that is all that concerns us. And that they are very apt to be sound on the practical matters of domestic and secular life, nothing but prejudice or self-conceit can prevent us from acknowledging. The inference, therefore, is unavoidable, that the man who thinks it beneath his dignity to take counsel with an intelligent wife, stands in his own light, and betrays that lack of judgment which he tacitly attributes to her.

As a general rule, wives confide the minutest of their plans and thoughts to their husbands, having no involvements to screen from them. Why not reciprocate, if but for the pleasure of meeting confidence with confidence? We are certain that no man succeeds so well in the world as he who, taking a partner for life, makes her the partner of his purposes and hopes. What is wrong of his impulse or judgment, she will check and set right with her almost universally right instincts. "Help-meet" was no insignificant title as applied to man's companion. She is a help-meet to him in every darkness, difficulty and sorrow of life. And what she most craves and most deserves is confidence—without which love is never free from a shadow.

XLII.

COURTESY.

WE do not hesitate to claim for courtesy, as Doctor Johnson did for cleanliness, a place among the virtues. It is a virtue, and one which greatly promotes the comfort and happiness of mankind. It is the sugar in the cup of life—the sweetener of domestic and social existence. The very name of this grace is so associated with the stiff, frigid, and, in some instances, ludicrous forms of etiquette, that we are apt to overlook its worth, and have inadequate ideas of its importance. These forms, unless they be all the more extravagant, are by no means to be neglected; but it should not be forgotten that they are often punctiliously observed by persons who do not know what real politeness is—in whose minds the sentiments that create true courtesy have no place.

To be courteous in the best sense, we must have an humble estimate of ourselves and our attainments. Excessive vanity and true politeness will not be found together. When you meet with a person who is on the very best terms with himself, and has a very extravagant idea of his own importance, you need not expect to receive very courteous or respectful treatment from him. It can scarcely have escaped the notice of the least observing, that the artificial manners current in society are constructed in deference to the sentiment of humility.

"The tendency of pride," says one of the greatest and best of men, "to produce strife and hatred is sufficiently apparent from the pains men have been at to construct a system of politeness, which is nothing more than a sort of mimic humility, in which the sentiments of an offensive self-estimation are so far disguised and suppressed as to make them compatible with the spirit of society; such a mode of behavior as would naturally result from an attention to the apostolic injunction, 'Let nothing be done through strife or vain glory; but in lowliness of mind let each esteem others better than themselves;'" and if even the hollow forms of this virtue be so important that we cannot dispense with them, how much more valuable must the reality be; if the painting be both useful and pleasing, how excellent and charming the original! Humility, then, it should be kept in mind, is essential to genuine courtesy. The really humble individual will not usurp a place to which he has no claim. He will be content with his own share, or rather less, in conversation. Even when conscious of being in the right, he will not express his convictions in that rude and boisterous tone, which creates disgust both at the speaker and what he says; he will not state his views as if they were so many self-evident axioms, reminding wise and sensible listeners of the taunt of a venerable Scripture worthy, "No doubt but ye are the people, and wisdom shall die with you." He will beware of exalting himself above others; of hinting even indirectly their inferiority to him. He will not take the faults and misfortunes of others as incense to his own vanity—a practice which, though common, is mean and despicable. It is easy to see how an humble opinion of one's self will thus promote genuine politeness.

Affectionateness is another of its essential prerequisites. To be pleasingly well-bred, we must have a regard for those with whom we mingle; for its absence no artificial deference will compensate. The great desire of every person when he goes into society, should be to contribute as largely as possible to the general fund of happiness—to impart as well as receive pleasure. Good will toward all with whom we feel it right to associate, must shine through the countenance, flow from the tongue, be conveyed in the cordial grasp of the hand : and in a thousand ways, easier felt than described, be made apparent. Why should we blush to confess that we have a kindly feeling toward our fellow-creatures? Why seek to hide the sympathies that are so honorable to us? Why not circulate, as widely as we can, those feelings of brotherhood which are of such advantage to our race? There are some, indeed, who have so degraded themselves that they may be thought hardly entitled to affection. But even when called to mix with such persons, we should remember that kindness has a killing power, and that the best way to make a man respect himself, is to show that others would fain respect him, would he but act so as to enable them to do so. Affectionateness is indispensable to that kind of politeness which a man with a heart relishes. There is no mistaking cold artificial manners for the genuine courtesy of the heart. Persons with the gloomy and scowling look—the harsh, querulous, and domineering tone—on whose brows you can trace the clouds of the quarrel that was just hushed up as you crossed their threshold, never can be courteous in the best sense of the term. There is no good society, no circle worth spending an hour in, where love is not a guest. Her presence is indispensable to the "Feast of reason and the flow of soul."

A scrupulous and delicate regard to the feelings of others, is also an essential ingredient in the character of a well-bred person. The most guarded, indeed, may occasionally trespass through ignorance or inattention, but they who do so designedly violate the first law of correct manners, which is to make all around us feel as easy and cheerful as possible. There are some persons so sensitive and touchy on almost every topic, whose sensitiveness, too, arises from their overweening self-conceit, that one can scarcely be expected so to shape his speech as not to give them offense; while there are those who have so little regard for the feelings of others, that we almost feel it a duty, when an opportunity occurs, to send them a pretty hard blow in return. We quite agree with the sentiment of one of the greatest of moralists, "They who cannot take a jest ought not to make one." These exceptions apart, however, there is such a thing as wantonly tampering with the feelings of those with whom we mingle, which is one of the grossest outrages upon good breeding. If the gentle Cowper was right when he said that he would not enter upon the list of his friends, the man who would heedlessly set foot upon a worm, what are we to say of those who intentionally would crush or wound that sensitive, and sprightly, and loving thing, the human heart? They should be sent to herd alone. They are the kind of natures whom one would be glad to see betake themselves to the cloister or the cave; they are among the nuisances of the social circle, the banes of domestic life. Higher motives apart, self-love should prevent such conduct. Who is altogether invulnerable? Is not that individual singularly fortunate—the rare exception—who has nothing in his personal appearance, habits, profession, past history, present condition, family connections, and the like, fitted when an uncourteous and unfeeling allusion is made to it, to stir a sigh or kindle a blush? And every man is aware when such allusions in his own case would be felt cruel, and he should not forget to act toward his neighbor on the golden maxim, "Do unto others as you would have others do unto you."

A prying and inquisitive disposition, too, is incompatible with true politeness. Impertinent curiosity is one of the chief banes of social intercourse. It is easy to see how it becomes so. You put a question respecting circumstances which you have no right to know anything about, and which common sense might tell you the party you interrogate is not willing to disclose. The latter must either equivocate or directly falsify, or, much to the annoyance of his own feelings, state distinctly that the question is one you have no right to put, and which, therefore, he does not mean to answer. So that if to preserve tranquillity of mind, to impart as well as to receive pleasure, be the object of good manners, every Paul Pry in the social circle must be a very offensive person indeed. We should keep a "sharp look-out" on those whose conversation is chiefly in the question form.

True courtesy has other elements, on which we do not enlarge at present. There is, for example, purity of conversation—that purity which teaches us to shun not merely open obscenity, but what is often as dangerous— covert insinuation. Then there is the propriety of feeling as much at ease as may be consistent with due respect to others. "Ease," Lord Chesterfield says, "is the standard of politeness." We must be courteous to those beneath our own roof, would we practice this grace in society. We may rest assured that politeness is a grace of no mean order. Some may affect to contemn it;—it says the less for their sense, their taste, their virtue. That man has need of far more merit than falls to the share of ordinary mortals, who dares to act in contravention of the established forms and usages of society; and even the most accomplished in mind will be all the better that they be accomplished in manners too. It is a vulgar error that a man will scarcely be a *genius*, and at the same time a *gentleman.*

How much a sincere and hearty politeness may do for others, is readily tested and measured by all who have learned to appreciate it for themselves. While it is comparatively easy to be courteous toward strangers, or toward people of distinction, whom one meets in society or on public occasions, still it should be remembered that it is at home, in the family, and among kindred, that an every-day politeness of manners is really most to be prized. There it confers substantial benefits, and brings the sweetest returns. The little attentions which members of the same household may show toward one another day by day belong, in fact, to what is styled "good breeding." There cannot be any ingrained gentility which does not exhibit itself first at home. There, of all places in the world, it will be able to demonstrate how much genuine politeness there is in the heart. A well-ordered family cannot afford to dispense with the observance of the good rules of mutual intercourse which are enforced in good society. A churlish, sour, morose deportment at home is simply cruel, for it cuts into the tenderest sensibilities and hurts love just where love is strongest and most loyal. Parents and children, brothers and sisters, husbands and wives, never lose anything by mutual politeness; on the contrary, by maintaining not only its forms, but by the inward cultivation of its spirit, they become contributors to that domestic felicity which is, in itself, a foretaste of heaven.

No pleasanter sight is there, than a family of young folks who are quick to perform little acts of attention toward their elders. The placing of the big arm-chair for mamma, running for a footstool for aunty, hunting up papa's spectacles, and scores of little deeds, show the tender sympathy of gentle loving hearts; but if mamma never returns a smiling "Thank you, dear;" if papa's "Just what I was wanting, Susie," does not indicate that the little attention is appreciated, the children soon drop the habit. Little people are imitative creatures, and quickly catch the spirit surrounding them. So if, when the mother's spool of cotton rolls from her lap, the father stoops to pick it up, bright eyes will see the act, and quick minds make a note of it. By example, a thousand times more quickly than by precept, can children be taught to speak kindly to each other, to acknowledge favors, to be gentle and unselfish, to be thoughtful and considerate of the comfort of the family. The boys, with inward pride of their father's courteous demeanor, will be chivalrous and helpful to their young sisters; the girls, imitating their mother, will be patient and gentle, even when big brothers are noisy and heedless. In the homes where true courtesy prevails, it seems to meet you on the threshold. You feel the kindly welcome on entering. No angry voices are heard up-stairs. No sullen children are sent from the room. No peremptory orders are given to cover the delinquencies of house-keeping or servants. A delightful atmosphere pervades the house —unmistakable, yet indescribable.

Such a house, filled by the spirit of love, is a home indeed to all who enter within its consecrated walls.

Speak kindly in the morning; it lightens the cares of the day, and makes the household and all other affairs move along more smoothly.

Speak kindly at night, for it may be that before the dawn some loved one may finish his or her space of life, and it will be too late to ask forgiveness.

Speak kindly at all times; it encourages the downcast, cheers the sorrowing, and very likely awakens the erring to earnest resolves to do better, with strength to keep them.

Kind words are balm to the soul. They oil up the entire machinery of life, and keep it in good running order.

XLIII.

HOME GOVERNMENT.

THE importance of sacredly guarding the family relation cannot well be overestimated. It is the foundation-stone of all that is good and pure both in civilization and religion. Take this away, and the whole fabric must topple and fall. Would you look into the future as with the spirit of prophecy, and read as with a telescope the history and character of our country, and of other countries? You have but to watch the eyes of children at play.

What children are, neighborhoods are. What neighborhoods are, communities are,—states, empires, worlds! They are the elements of Hereafter made visible.

They are the flowers of the invisible world, —indestructible, self-perpetuating flowers, with each a multitude of angels and evil spirits underneath its leaves, toiling and wrestling for dominion over it! They are the blossoms of another world, whose fruitage is angels and archangels. They are dew-drops that have their source, not in the chambers of the earth, nor among the vapors of the sky.

The very tones of the voice they last listened to make an impression upon their sensitive organizations. Mothers, do not think the time and strength wasted, which you spend in reviewing the day with your little boy or girl; do not neglect to teach it how to pray, and pray for it in simple and earnest language, which it can understand. Soothe and quiet its little heart after the experiences of the day. It has had its disappointments and trials as well as its play and pleasures; it is ready to throw its arms around your neck, and take its good-night kiss.

Always send your little child to bed happy. Whatever cares may trouble your mind, give the dear child a warm good-night kiss as it goes to its pillow. The memory of this, in the stormy years which may be in store for the little one, will be like Bethlehem's star to the bewildered shepherds; and welling up in the heart will rise the thought: "My father, my mother—*loved me!*" Lips parched with fever will become dewy again at this thrill of useful memories. Kiss your little child before it goes to sleep.

Always allow them to tell you all that has happened to interest or annoy them while absent from home. Never think anything which affects the happiness of your children too small a matter to claim your attention. Use every means in your power to win and retain their confidence. Do not rest satisfied without some account of each day's joys or sorrows. It is a source of great comfort to the innocent child to tell all its troubles to mother, and do you lend a willing ear. For know you, that as soon as they cease to tell you all these things, they have chosen other confidants, and therein lies the danger. O mother! this is the rock on which your son may be wrecked at last. I charge you to set a watch upon it. Be jealous of the first sign that he is not opening all his heart to you.

Government is not to watch children with a suspicious eye, to frown at the merry outbursts of innocent hilarity, to suppress their joyous laughter, and to mould them into melancholy little models of octogenarian gravity. And when they have been in fault, it is not simply to punish them on acount of the personal injury that you have chanced to suffer in consequence of their fault, while disobedience, unattended by inconvenience to yourself, passes without notice.

Reprove with calmness and composure, and not with angry irritation,—in a few words, fitly chosen, and not with a torrent of abuse; punish as often as you threaten, and threaten only when you intend and can remember to perform; say what you mean, and infallibly do as you say.

It is a great mistake to suppose that what will make a child stare or tremble impresses more authority. The violent emphasis, the hard, stormy voice, the menacing air, only weaken authority. Is it not well understood, that a bawling and violent teamster has no real government over his team? Is it not practically seen that a skillful commander of one of those huge floating cities, moved by steam on our American waters, manages and works every motion by the waving of the hand, or by signs that pass in silence, issuing no order at all, save in the gentlest undertone of voice? So when there is, or is to be, a real order in the house, it will come of no hard and boisterous, or fretful and termagant way of commanding. Gentleness will speak the word of firmness, and firmness will be clothed in that of true gentleness.

Good moral habits are essential to the healthfulness of the home; and these may be best taught by the watchful mother's training. One important part of her work is to remove *hindrances* out of her children's way to health and happiness. No dirt, or dirty habits, for example, should be permitted. Washing their hands and faces many times in the day will often remove a sense of discomfort which makes them fretful, as also will giving them food at regular periods. Ragged dress, too, and broken fastenings, add a feeling of degradation, that a careful mother will prevent as far as possible by keeping their clothes whole, neat, and clean. Making their own garments, we may here remark, gives useful employment to girls, and is an important aid in training them to thrifty habits. Many families go in rags because they never learned to sew; while the same wages in the hands of those who know how to employ that useful "one-eyed servant," the needle, keep the household looking always respectable.

Never scold children, but soberly and quietly reprove. Do not employ shame except in extreme cases. The suffering is acute; it hurts self-respect in the child to reprove a child before the family; to ridicule it, to tread down its feelings ruthlessly, is to wake in its bosom malignant feelings. A child is defenceless; he is not allowed to argue. He is often tried, condemned, and executed in a second. He finds himself of little use. He is put at things he don't care for, and withheld from things which he does like. He is made the convenience of grown-up people; is hardly supposed to have any rights, except in a corner, as it were; is sent hither and thither; made to get up or sit down for everybody's convenience but his own; is snubbed and catechised until he learns to dodge government and elude authority, and then be whipped for being "such a liar that no one can believe you."

Parents often speak of breaking the will of a child; but it seems to us they had better break its neck. The will needs regulating, not destroying. We should as soon think of breaking the legs of a horse in training him, as a child's will. We never yet heard of a will in itself too strong, more than of an arm too mighty, or a mind too comprehensive in its grasp, or too powerful in its hold. We would discipline and develop the will into harmonious proportions. The instruction of a child should be such as to animate, inspire and train, but not to hew, cut and carve; for we should always treat a child as a live tree, which was to be helped to grow; never as dry, dead timber, to be carved into this or that shape, and have certain grooves cut in it. A living tree, and not dead timber, is every little child.

Mothers, don't whip them! Treat God's lambs tenderly. Compel obedience, but not with the rod. The other evening the maternal face appeared at the door of a pleasant little home I had often noticed, and loudly ordered a little lad of three or so to " come in and see if she did not do as she said she would." The mother, in her wrath at being disobeyed, re entered the house, not hearing the little one's sobbing explanation that he had stepped outside to bring the baby in. Directly the blows and piteous cries fell upon my ears. Undoubtedly the little one had gone beyond the prescribed bounds; but it was to bring the wee toddling thing inside, who as yet heeded not commands, however harshly given, and his full heart and meagre use of words withheld the power of explanation. Poor little man, how my heart ached for him! Kissless and sad he went to bed. Mothers, do not whip them! Do not yourselves make shadows in the sunlight with which God always surrounds children. Do not let them be lulled to sleep by the falling of their tears, or by their own sad sobs and sighs. Far pleasanter it is when you go to tuck them in at night, to find pink feet on the pillow, dimpled knees in air, toys yet in embrace and smiles on their sweet mouths. Yourselves bear in mind their last words, "If I should die before I wake." Treat them tenderly. I took my little man a shot-gun to-night, handing it over the gate, I said, " Now will you mind your mamma, and stay inside when she tells you?" I am sure the "me will" was very sincere; but if they forget, bear with them. If childhood's days cannot be free from sorrow, surely none ever may.

They will not trouble you long. Children grow up—nothing on earth grows so fast as children. It was but yesterday, and that lad was playing with tops, a buoyant boy. He is a man, and gone now! There is no more childhood for him or for us. Life has claimed him. When a beginning is made, it is like a raveling stocking; stitch by stitch gives way till all are gone. The house has not a child in it—there is no more noise in the hall—boys rushing in pell-mell; it is very orderly now. There are no more skates or sleds, bats, balls or strings left scattered about. Things are neat enough now. There is no delay for sleepy folks; there is no longer any task, before you lie down, of looking after anybody, and tucking up the bedclothes. There are no disputes to settle, nobody to get off to school, no complaint, no importunities for impossible things, no rips to mend, no fingers to tie up, no faces to be washed, or collars to be arranged. There never was such peace in the house! It would sound like music to have some feet clatter down the front stairs! Oh for some children's noise! What used to ail us, that we were hushing their loud laugh, checking their noisy frolic, and reproving their slamming and banging the doors? We wish our neighbors would only lend us an urchin or two to make a little noise in these premises. A home without children! It is like a lantern and no candle; a garden and no flowers; a vine and no grapes; a brook and no water gurgling and gushing in its channel. We want to be tired, to be vexed, to be run over, to hear children at work with all its varieties. During the secular days, this is enough marked. But it is the Sabbath that puts our homes to the proof. That is the Christian family day. The intervals of public worship are long spaces of peace. The family seems made up on that day. The children are at home. You can lay your hands upon their heads. They seem to recognize the greater and lesser love—to God and to friends. The house is peaceful, but not still. There is a low and melodious thrill of children in it. But the

Sabbath comes too still now. There is a silence that aches in the ear. There is too much room at the table, too much at the hearth. The bedrooms are a world too orderly. There is too much leisure and too little care. Alas! what mean these things? Is somebody growing old? Are these signs and tokens? Is life waning?

XLIV.

BROKEN TIES.

HOW many there are in every human experience! How many even apart from those that death occasions! Your memory goes back to the home of your childhood. All its belongings became, as it were, a part of your nature. You recall the familiar surroundings. Your interests were bound up with them. And then the time came when those ties must be sundered. You went forth from the old home into new scenes. You found these ties binding themselves about you, but the old ones were broken.

And so it has been all the way along. You became attached to persons and the shifting scenes of life have carried them away from you, and though you hear now and then of their well-being, the old intimacy is perforce gone, the old ties are sundered. The ties that hold us to our surroundings are continually breaking. No year is like that which preceded it, no month, no day even.

Let us guard against those things that may give offense, or that may through any fault of ours break the tie that binds us to an old friend. There is the bitterness of parting and the added bitterness of self-reproach, the sad recollection of what might have been.

And, since all things and relations change, since ties must be broken, it is well for us to learn to enjoy to the utmost our present. The time is coming when your home ties perhaps must be sundered. Enjoy, then, the present relations. It may be a humble home, and you are planning for one larger, and, to your imagination, more enjoyable. Very well; only do not fail to take all the enjoyment you can from your present surroundings. Your friend will go to some distant place by and by. Enjoy his society while you have it. Your children, while they will always be your children, will nevertheless grow up and go out from the home-nest. The ties that bind you to their youth will be severed. Enjoy them while you have them with you. It is well for us to plan as wisely as may be for the future; but it is folly for us to seek our enjoyment in the future. Let us enjoy what we have now, for "change" is written on all our transitory and mutable life. It will be only when we have sundered the last bonds that bind us to this life that we shall be where there is no more breaking of ties, no more regrets over pleasures that are gone, but sweet enjoyment of an eternal present.

XLV.

BREVITY OF LIFE.

LIKE to the falling of a star,
Or as the flights of eagles are,
Or like the fresh spring's gaudy hue,
Or silver drops of morning dew,
Or like a wind that chafes the flood,
Or bubbles which on water stood—
E'en such is man, whose borrowed light
Is straight called in, and paid to-night.
The wind blows out, the bubble dies,
The spring entombed in autumn lies,
The dew dries up, the star is shot,
The flight is past—and man forgot!

A LITTLE while ago we were not in the world—a little while hence we shall be here no longer. This is arithmetic. This is the clock. Demosthenes used to say that every speech should begin with an incontrovertible proposition. Now, it is scientifically incontrovertible that a little while ago, we were not here, and a little while hence we shall be here no more.

How distinctly we remember longing for the time when we should be eighteen or twenty years old; how long the time seemed then; how short as we look back upon it. Ask any aged person how long since he or she was a child, and the answer will be, "it seems but as yesterday."

Old age is honorable, and a multitude of years teach wisdom. How pleasant to converse with the aged of the times fifty, threescore, or even threescore and ten years since. Some young people, children and grand-children, are impatient of old age, while others have a filial delight in their company, and love to care for them, and tenderly lessen their burdens. Old age, however serene the conscience and well-spent the life, has its sadness. After all their care and toil, the provision they have made for themselves, and children on whom they wish to lean in the decline of life, they have a dread and fear of being a burden.

If you would make the aged happy, lead them to feel that there is still a place for them where they can be useful. When you see their powers failing, do not notice it. It is enough for them to feel it, without a reminder. Do not humiliate them by doing things after them. Accept their offered services, and do not let them *see you* taking off the dust their poor eye-sight has left undisturbed, or wiping up the liquid their trembling hands have spilled; rather let the dust remain, and the liquid stain the carpet, than rob them of their self-respect by *seeing you* cover their deficiencies. You may give them the best room in your house, you may garnish it with pictures, and flowers, you may yield them the best seat in your church-pew, the easiest chair in your parlor, the highest seat of honor at your table; but if you *lead*, or *leave*, them to feel that they have passed their usefulness, you plant a thorn in their bosom that will rankle there while life lasts. If they are capable of doing nothing but preparing your kindlings, or darning your stockings, indulge them in those things, but never let them feel that it is because they can do nothing else; rather that they do this so well.

Do not ignore their taste and judgment. It may be that in their early days, and in the circle where they move, they were as much sought and honored as you are now; and until you arrive at that place, you can ill imagine your feelings should you be considered entirely void of their qualities, be regarded as essential to no one, and your opinions be unsought, or discarded if given. They *may* have been active and successful in the training of children and youth in the way they should go ; and will they not feel it keenly, if no attempt is made to draw from this rich experience?

Indulge them as far as possible in their old habits. The various forms of society in which they were educated may be as dear to them as yours are now to you ; and can they see them slighted or disowned without a pang? If they relish their meals better by turning their tea into the saucer, having their butter on the same plate with their food, or eating with both knife and fork, do not in word or deed imply to them that the customs of their days are obnoxious in good society ; and that they are stepping down from respectability as they *descend* the hill-side of life. Always bear in mind that the customs of which you are now so tenacious may be equally repugnant to the next generation.

It cannot be that earth is man's only abiding place. It cannot be that our life is a bubble, cast up by the ocean of eternity, to float another moment upon its surface, and then sink into nothingness and darkness forever. Else why is it that the high and glorious aspirations which leap like angels from the temples of our hearts, are forever wandering abroad, unsatisfied?

Why is it that the rainbow and the cloud come over us with a beauty that is not of earth, and then pass off and leave us to muse on their faded loveliness?

Why is it that the stars which hold their festival around the midnight throne are set above the grasp of our limited faculties, and are forever mocking us with their unapproachable glory?

Finally, why is it that bright forms of human beauty are presented to the view, and then taken from us, leaving the thousand streams of the affections to flow back in an Alpine torrent upon our hearts?

We are born for a higher destiny than that of earth. There is a realm where the rainbow never fades; where the stars will be spread out before us like the islands that slumber on the ocean; and where the beautiful beings that here pass before us like visions will stay in our presence forever!

XLVI.

THE SILENT SHORE.

THE beautiful have gone with their bloom from the gaze of human eyes. Soft eyes that made it springtime to our hearts are seen no more. We have loved the light of many a smile that has faded from us now; and in our hearts have lingered sweet voices that now are hushed in the silence of death. Seats are left vacant in our earthly homes, which none again can fill. Kindred and friends, loved ones, have passed away one by one; our hearts are left desolate; we are lonely without them. They have passed with their love to "that land, from whose bourne no traveler returns." Shall we never see them again? Memory turns with lingering regret to recall those smiles and the loved tone of those dear familiar voices. In fancy they are often by our side, but their home is

on a brighter shore. They visit us in our dreams, floating over our memory like shadows over moonlit waters. When the heart is weary with anguish, and the soul is bowed with grief, do they not come and whisper thoughts of comfort and hope? Yes, sweet memory brings them to us, and the love we bore them lifts the heart from earthly aspirations, and we long to join them in that better land.

We may feel sad because they are lost to us; but while we weep and wonder, they are wrapped in garments of light, and warble songs of celestial joy. They will return to us no more; but we shall go to them; share their pleasures; emulate their sympathies; and compete with them in the path of endless development. We would not call them back. In the homes above they are great, and well-employed and blest. Shadows fall upon them no more; nor is life ruffled with anxious cares; love rules their life and thoughts; and eternal hopes beckon them forever to the pursuit of infinite good.

To whom are these thoughts strange and dull? Who has no treasure in Heaven—well-remembered forms hallowed by separation and distance—stars of hope illumining with ever increasing beauty life's utmost horizon? What family circle has remained unbroken —no empty chair—no cherished mementoes— voices and footsteps returning no more—no members transferred to the illimitable beyond? Where is he who has stood unhurt amid the chill blasts, that have blighted mortal hopes, and withered mortal loves? Alas! the steps of death are everywhere; his voice murmuring in every sweep of the wind; his ruins visible on towering hill and in sequestered vale. We all have *felt* or *seen* his power. Beneath the cypress we rest and weep; our hearts riven with memories of the loved and lost; and yet hope springing eternal from earth's mausoleums to penetrate and possess the future.

Faith penetrates the veil, and bids the invisible stand disclosed; while its magic wand wakens into life forms well-known, but holier and lovelier far than we knew them here. Such thoughts make us better, purer, gentler. We cannot keep society with the sainted dead, and with the great God in whose presence they dwell, without feeling a nobler life throbbing through us. They draw us upward. We grow less earthly, more heavenly; and God-like aspirations come to us, as we wander along the border land where dwell the sainted dead.

"The sorrow for the dead," says Irving, "is the only sorrow from which we refuse to be divorced. Every other wound we seek to heal, every other affliction to forget; but this wound we consider it a duty to keep open; this affliction we cherish and brood over in solitude.

"Where is the mother who would willingly forget the infant that perished like a blossom from her arms, though every recollection is a pang? Where is the child that would willingly forget the most tender of parents, though to remember be but to lament? Who, even in the hour of agony, would forget the friend over whom he mourns? Who, even when the tomb is closing upon the remains of her he most loved, when he feels his heart, as it were, crushed in the closing of its portal, would accept of consolation that must be bought by forgetfulness?

"No; the love which survives the tomb is one of the noblest attributes of the soul. If it has its woes, it has likewise its delights; and when the overwhelming burst of grief is calmed into the gentle tear of recollection, when the sudden anguish and the convulsive agony over the ruins of all we most loved is softened away into pensive meditation on all that it was in the days of its loveliness, who would root out such a sorrow from the heart?

"Though it may sometimes throw a passing cloud over the bright hour of gayety, or spread a deeper sadness over the hour of gloom, yet who would exchange it even for the song of pleasure or the burst of revelry? No; there is a voice from the tomb sweeter than song. There is a remembrance of the dead to which we turn even from the charms of the living.

"Oh, the grave! the grave! It buries every error, covers every defect, extinguishes every resentment. From its peaceful bosom spring none but fond regrets and tender recollections. Who can look upon the grave even of an enemy, and not feel a compunctious throb that he should ever have warred with the poor handful of earth that lies mouldering before him?

"But the grave of those we loved, what a place for meditation! There it is that we call up in long review the whole history of virtue and gentleness, and the thousand endearments lavished upon us almost unheeded in the daily intercourse of intimacy. There it is that we dwell upon the tenderness, the solemn, awful tenderness of the parting scene.

"The bed of death, with all its stifled griefs, its noiseless attendants, its mute, watchful assiduities, the last testimonies of expiring love, the feeble, fluttering, thrilling, oh, how thrilling! pressure of the hand. The last fond look of the glazing eye, turning upon us even from the threshold of existence. The faint, faltering accents struggling in death to give one more assurance of affection. Aye, go to the grave of buried love and meditate! There settle the account with thy conscience for every past benefit unrequited, every past endearment unregarded, of that departed being who can never—never—never return to be soothed by thy contrition!

"If thou art a child, and hast ever added a sorrow to the soul or a furrow to the silver brow of an affectionate parent; if thou art a husband, and hast ever caused the fond bosom that ventured its whole happiness in thy arms to doubt one moment of thy kindness or thy truth ; if thou art a friend, and hast ever wronged, in thought, or word, or deed, the spirit that generously confided in thee ; if thou art a lover, and hast given one unmerited pang to that true heart which now lies cold and still beneath thy feet ; then be sure every unkind look, every ungracious word, every ungentle action, will come thronging back upon thy memory, and knocking dolefully at thy soul ; then be sure that thou wilt lie down sorrowing and repentant on the grave, and utter the unheard groan, and pour the unavailing tear, more deep, more bitter, because unheard and unavailing.

"Then weave thy chaplet of flowers, and strew the beauties of nature about the grave ; console thy broken spirit, if thou canst, with these tender, yet futile tributes of regret; but take warning by the bitterness of this thy contrite affliction over the dead, and henceforth be more faithful and affectionate in the discharge of thy duties to the living."

When we are dead, there will be some

honest sorrow. A few will be really sad, as we are robed for the grave. Fewer, probably, than we now suppose. We are vain enough to think our departure will produce considerable sensation. But we over-estimate it. Out of a small circle how soon shall we be forgotten! A single leaf of a boundless forest has fallen! That is all.

> "The gay will laugh
> When thou art gone; the solemn brood of care
> Plod on; and each one, as before, will chase
> His favorite phantom."

When we are dead, affection may erect a monument. But the hand that set it up will soon be as powerless as ours, and for the same cause. How soon they that weep over us will follow us! The monument itself will crumble, and it will fall on the dust that covers us. If the marble or the granite long endures, yet the eye of affection will not endure to read the graven letters. Men will give a glance at the name of one they never knew, and pass on with not a thought of the slumberer below.

Deplorable indeed, is the state of him, who,

having run through life's brief years in the sweet sunshine of comfort and earthly happiness, comes at length to the unwelcome hour when Death summons him away, and who, as he glances his spirit's eye through the vast future that awaits him, sees no cheering light, no rising sun, to gladden his endless career, and remembers, with bitterness of soul, that although he has rejoiced in many years upon the earth, many, many "days of darkness" now lie before him, even an Eternity of sorrow and unavailing repentance.

Thrice happy he, whose path is that of the just, which, beaming brighter and brighter day by day, is lost at length in the noontide splendors of the Heavenly Glory!

www.ingramcontent.com/pod-product-compliance
Lightning Source LLC
Chambersburg PA
CBHW020544300426
44111CB00008B/783